PORTUGUESE SHORT STORIES FOR BEGINNERS

20 Captivating Short Stories to Learn Brazilian Portuguese & Grow Your Vocabulary the Fun Way!

Easy Portuguese Stories

Lingo Mastery

www.LingoMastery.com

ISBN: 9781097423613

Free Book Reveals The 6 Step Blueprint That Took Students **From Language Learners To Fluent In 3 Months**

- **6 Unbelievable Hacks** that will accelerate your learning curve

- **Mind Training:** why memorizing vocabulary is easy

- **One Hack To Rule Them All:** This secret nugget will blow you away...

Head over to **LingoMastery.com/hacks** and claim your free book now!

CONTENTS

INTRODUCTION

So, you want to learn Portuguese? That's awesome! Portuguese is a beautiful language spoken by over 250 million people across the world, being the mother tongue in amazing countries such as Brazil, Portugal, Cape Verde, etc., and even in Macau, a city in China! It is a language that has spread across every continent and which opens the doors to entire worlds once you learn how to speak it.

Portuguese is a very old language, and its written form can be dated back to the 12th century. Vulgar Latin, which was spoken on the west coast of the Iberian Peninsula, (now Portugal and the Spanish province of Galicia) basically replaced all previous local languages. Vulgar Latin evolved into the Galician–Portuguese language. This then broke off into Galacian and Portuguese after the incorporation of Galicia into Spain and the independent development of Portugal.

It may be important to note at this point that having a basic to intermediate level of Portuguese may be an important tool for your professional future, as well as opening several doors for you on your resume if you feel the need to either migrate or work in a multi-cultural environment. Portuguse speakers will usually appreciate your effort in having partially or fully learned their language, and they will happily collaborate with you in solving your doubts.

What the following book is about

We've written this book to cover an important issue that seems to affect every new learner of the Portuguese language — a lack of helpful reading material. While in English you may encounter tons (or gigabytes, in our modern terms) of easy and accessible learning material, in Portuguese you will usually and promptly be given tough literature to read by your teachers, and you will soon find yourself consulting your dictionary more than you'd want to. Eventually, you'll find yourself bored and uninterested in continuing, and your initially positive outlook may soon turn sour.

There's something you must understand: Portuguese isn't an easy language, but it isn't a horribly difficult one either. You just need to make an effort in identifying your flaws and weaknesses and having purchased this book is a definite good start.

Our goal with this book will be to supply you with useful, entertaining, helpful and challenging material that will not only allow you to learn the language but also help you pass the time and make the experience less formal and more fun — like any particular lesson should be. We will not bore you with grammatical notes, spelling or structure: the book has been well-written and revised to ensure that it covers those aspects without having to explain them in unnecessarily complicated rules like text books do.

If you've ever learned a new language through conversational methods, teachers will typically just ask you to practice speaking. Here, we'll teach you writing and reading Portuguese with stories. You'll both learn how to read it *and* write it with the additional tools we'll give you at the end of each story.

How *Portuguese Short Stories for Beginners* has been laid out

We want to help you read stories and understand each aspect of the language in the most entertaining way, so we've compiled a series of tales which will each cover a tool of the language. Each story will tell a different tale involving unique, deep characters with their own personalities and conflicts, while ensuring that you understand the objective of the language device in Portuguese. Verbs, Pronouns, Nouns, Directions, Time and Date; all of it will be covered in this **Basic-level** book for **Beginners.** At no point will we introduce concepts too difficult for you to grasp, and any complicated vocabulary will be studied at the end of each story.

The stories have been written in a way that will allow you to:

a) Read the story without any distractions, paying attention solely to the plot of the tale without making special emphasis on distracting elements.

b) Interpret the tale you just read with the use of two summaries — one in English so that you may ensure you understood what the tale was about and can go back to it if there was something you didn't understand properly; and another in Portuguese for when you start to dominate the language a bit better, allowing you to create your own summary for the book later on.

c) Understand the related terms expressed throughout the story with the use of a list of vocabulary that will give you important definitions and clear up any doubts you may have acquired.

d) Finally: ensure you have understood what you've read by providing you with a list of simple-choice questions based on the story, with a list of answers below if you want to corroborate your choices.

All of this will ensure absolute efficiency in not only reading the stories, but in understanding and interpreting them once you're done. It is **normal** that you may find certain terms unknown to your knowledge of the language, and it is **equally normal** that sometimes you may ultimately not entirely understand what the story is about. We're here to *help* you, in any way we can.

Recommendations for readers of *Portuguese Short Stories for Beginners*

Before we allow you to begin reading, we have a quick list of recommendations, tips and tricks for getting the best out of this book.

1. Read the stories without any pressure: feel free to return to parts you didn't understand and take breaks when necessary. This is like any fantasy, romance or sci-fi book you'd pick up, except with different goals.

2. Feel free to use any external material to make your experience more complete: while we've provided you with plenty of data to help you learn, you may feel obliged to look at text books or search for more helpful texts on the internet — do not think twice about doing so! We even recommend it.

3. Find other people to learn with: while learning can be fun on your own, it helps to have friends or family joining you on the tough journey of learning a new language. Find a like-minded person to accompany you in this experience, and you may soon find yourself competing to see who can learn the most!

4. Try writing your own stories once you're done: all the material in this book is made for you to learn not only how to read, but how to write as well. Liked what you read? Try writing your own story now, and see what people think about it!

Well, with all of that said, we can finally begin with the book — after all, we want you to start reading our stories right away.

<u>Good luck, reader!</u>

CHAPTER ONE

BASIC VOCABULARY

Conhecendo uma nova cidade – Meeting a new city

É um dia de **sol**. Finalmente, eu (Mateus) e meus **amigos** (Pedro, João e Helena) vamos **viajar** juntos a um lugar que **sempre** quisemos ir. Nós somos **aventureiros** e gostamos de viajar e conhecer **lugares** novos. Adoramos mesmo escrever nossas próprias histórias.

Meus amigos fizeram um **convite** para visitar uma **cidade** do interior, localizada no estado brasileiro mais novo, o Tocantins. João, um **querido** amigo, nos lembra que ir ao **interior** é muito bom, **especialmente** para descansar e sair um pouco da vida agitada da capital.

Eu não **conheço** quase nada sobre a nova cidade, mas viajar de **carro** até lá vai ser **interessante**, pois vamos ver a paisagem mudar, observar **animais**, plantações, construções e contemplar a natureza.

A viagem começa e estamos **animados**, mesmo sabendo que vamos esperar algumas **horas** para chegar até o nosso destino. **Enquanto** Pedro dirige, eu converso com Helena, minha melhor amiga.

Vamos no carro de Pedro que é novo, uma pick-up 4x4 de cor prata, muito **confortável** e espaçosa. Pela estrada é possível ver árvores, plantações de soja, **milho**, feijão... **campos** vastos e o horizonte com muitas nuvens. O **tempo** está bom e o dia belo.

É um dia bem feliz para mim, porque estou fazendo uma das coisas que mais gosto: viajar e estar na companhia dos amigos. Eu não aguento ficar muito tempo em casa, mas **em breve** estarei de volta a minha **rotina**.

A **estrada** estava boa, sem muito **movimento**, então era **possível** observar tudo. Eu gosto da sensação de **liberdade** que viajar proporciona, além do mistério de não saber o que vou encontrar pelo caminho.

Helena consegue avistar alguns animais, **gado** nas fazendas com pasto, aves voando, e a **paisagem** vai mudando de campos abertos e pastos para mata fechada. Enquanto isso, Pedro conta para João sobre a **última** viagem que fez e ambos **concordam** que precisam fazer mais viagens juntos.

De repente, Pedro freia o carro bruscamente e desvia para a **pista** contrária.

"Pedro, o que aconteceu?" todos perguntamos. João olha para trás.

Pedro sabia que era **perigoso**, mas desviou de um animal **silvestre** que estava atravessando a pista, um Jabuti. Depois que o **susto** passa, Helena olha pelo retrovisor traseiro e faz um desejo de que o Jabuti atravesse logo a pista sem que seja **atropelado**.

Helena comenta que alguns países buscam **soluções** para minimizar o impacto do **homem** no meio ambiente e **explica** para nós o que são as "Pontes verdes" para animais em rodovias.

Pedro era filho de **fazendeiros** e estava acostumado a dirigir em estrada, mas também era **amante** dos animais e prezava por uma **convivência** harmônica.

Fazia muito tempo que eu queria ir ao Jalapão, mas sempre me faltava companhia e **informações**.

Fomos conversando sobre o fato de muita gente ter **preconceito** com destinos turísticos, **ecológicos**, de aventura, pois muitas vezes o **turista** é explorado. Alguns amigos de João fizeram esse mesmo **roteiro** recentemente e nos passaram algumas dicas para nossa viagem.

Todos falam que é um **destino** fantástico e que deixa aquela **sensação** de quero mais. Mas é uma viagem para quem não se importa com muitas horas de **caminhada**, esforço físico, aventuras e perigos. Não é como em qualquer outra.

Esta viagem aconteceu no **início** do mês e foram cinco dias no destino, pois também conhecemos a cidade de Palmas.

Ao longo da viagem fui **observando** que poucas pessoas fazem os passeios e percursos sozinhos, há outras **opções** para quem não quer **dirigir**.

Como fizemos a viagem com uma pick-up 4x4, Nissan Frontier, era **importante** que o motorista soubesse dirigir uma **caminhonete**, já que algumas estradas estão em condições ruins. Estávamos tranquilos, pois Pedro sabia dirigir muito bem em lugares assim.

É uma viagem que não pode ser feita em um carro **pequeno**, pois certamente o carro vai **estragar** ou não será possível chegar a todas as **atrações**. É preciso um veículo mais potente para trilhas e estradas de terra.

É preciso sair cedo para não pegar a estrada à noite. O **primeiro** percurso até Ponte Alta do Tocantins pode ter vários animais na pista à noite, então é bom evitar dirigir nesse **horário**. O percurso até o Jalapão é um semicírculo, sendo muito **prático** durante a viagem.

O primeiro hotel em que ficamos **hospedados** por três noites foi o Águas do Jalapão em Ponte Alta do Tocantins, que custou **cerca** de cento e setenta reais por casal por dia. Ele tem o próprio **restaurante** e é preciso fazer uma reserva da refeição.

É importante levar alguma quantidade de **dinheiro em espécie**, pois a maioria dos lugares não passa cartão.

O segundo lugar em que ficamos uma noite foi a Pousada Monte Videl, em Mateiros. Nós jantamos no restaurante do Bob que é **bem conhecido** e o melhor, **de acordo** com a opinião do pessoal.

O terceiro lugar em que ficamos foi a pousada Cachoeiras do Jalapão, em São Félix do Tocantins. Eles **também** têm restaurante próprio, mas é preciso pedir com **antecedência**. A comida é simples, porém vem com fartura e é muito **gostosa**.

Eu lembro que as **pousadas** também tinham um excelente **café da manhã**. Helena adorou, pois ela tem muita fome pela manhã e gosta de tomar um café da manhã reforçado para ter a **energia** necessária para fazer as **trilhas**.

No primeiro dia saímos da Ponte Alta do Tocantins por volta de 7 e meia da manhã. Fomos à Lagoa do Japonês, um lugar **lindo**, de águas cristalinas com **pedras** ao fundo, refletindo **cores** belíssimas. Este é um ótimo lugar para **mergulhar**. Usamos umas sapatilhas de mergulho.

Almoçamos às 13 horas no restaurante da dona Maria, tivemos que deixar reservado antes, mas ficou pronto na hora e a comida estava muito gostosa, tudo bem limpinho.

Mais tarde, vimos o **pôr do sol** na Pedra Furada, um **espetáculo** com a presença de araras azuis que, inclusive, são raras. Assim que o sol se pôs, voltamos para Ponte Alta.

No segundo dia tomamos o café da manhã reforçado do hotel, pois o dia seria muito **pesado**. Arrumamos todas as nossas **bagagens** e saímos às 8:30h da manhã, levamos comidas e **lanches**, pois provavelmente não teríamos como almoçar, já que o caminho era muito longo e passamos muitas horas andando de carro.

Finalmente chegamos e fomos visitar a Cachoeira da Velha. A estrada que é bem ruim e longa cerca de vinte e nove quilômetros para ir e mais vinte e nove quilômetros para voltar, mas é realmente **impressionante**.

Adoramos a **vista** e a **umidade**. É possível sentar nas pedras e observar a beleza das **quedas d'água** branquinhas

Depois fomos à **praia** que se forma após o **rio** e nos refrescamos bastante antes de voltar. Pedro, João e eu fizemos um rafting bem emocionante. Helena ficou com **medo**, mas fez várias fotos nossas.

Depois foi a nossa vez de conhecer as Dunas. Todos vão para **assistir** o pôr do sol. Chegamos lá às 16h50, quase na hora de fechar (17:00). Dez minutos depois não entraríamos mais. Ainda bem! O pôr do sol nas Dunas é fantástico!

Helena não gostou muito porque ficou **preocupada** com as **abelhas**. Descobrimos que para evitar chamar a atenção delas é preciso não usar **perfumes**, cremes com fragrância e roupas amarelas ou laranja.

Nos dois últimos dias, visitamos vários outros lugares, mas gostamos mesmo de conhecer os fervedouros, pequenos lagos com **águas cristalinas** formadas de uma **nascente** subterrânea na qual sai uma grande quantidade de água misturada com **areia**.

Os fervedouros são tão **incríveis** que parecem não ser de verdade. As cores dos fervedouros são **fantásticas**, a água é cristalina. Nós fomos em cinco fervedouros, mas tem muito mais. E as águas em todas as atrações são de uma **transparência** impressionante.

Voltamos para Palmas onde iríamos **dormir** e no dia seguinte pegar a estrada de volta para casa. Foi uma aventura incrível e tiramos várias **fotos** para lembrar destes dias **ao lado de** nossos amigos.

Resumo da história

Quem nunca passou por situações que valem a pena contar? Mateus, Pedro, João e Helena foram conhecer uma nova cidade no Tocantins. Entre as aventuras, conheceram muitos pontos turísticos novos e lugares de natureza exuberante, paz e tranquilidade que um lugar de interior pode oferecer.

Summary of the story

Who has never had situations that are worth telling? Matthew, Peter, John and Helen went to see a new city in Tocantins. Among the adventures, they have met many new sights and places of lush nature, peace and tranquility that the countryside can offer.

Vocabulary

- **sol:** sun
- **amigos:** friends
- **viajar:** travel
- **sempre:** always
- **aventureiros:** adventurers
- **convite:** invitation
- **cidade:** city
- **querido:** dear
- **interior:** countryside
- **especialmente:** particularly
- **conheço:** know
- **carro:** car
- **interessante:** interesting
- **animais:** animals
- **animados:** excited
- **horas:** hours
- **enquanto:** while
- **confortável:** comfortable
- **árvores:** trees
- **milho:** corn
- **campos:** fields
- **tempo:** weather
- **em breve:** soon
- **rotina:** routine
- **estrada:** road
- **movimento:** movement
- **possível:** possible
- **liberdade:** freedom
- **gado:** cattle
- **paisagem:** landscape
- **última:** last
- **concordam:** agree
- **pista:** lane
- **perigoso:** dangerous
- **silvestre:** wild
- **susto:** scare
- **atropelado:** ran over
- **soluções:** solutions
- **homem:** man
- **explica:** explain
- **fazendeiros:** farmers
- **amante:** lover
- **convivência:** coexistence
- **informações:** information
- **preconceito:** prejudice
- **ecológicos:** ecological
- **turista:** tourist
- **roteiro:** tour
- **destino:** destination
- **sensação:** sensation
- **caminhada:** walk
- **início:** beginning
- **observando:** observing

- **opções:** options
- **dirigir:** drive
- **importante:** important
- **caminhonete:** truck
- **pequeno:** small
- **estragar:** spoil
- **atrações:** attractions
- **primeiro:** first
- **horário:** time
- **prático:** practical
- **hospedados:** hosted
- **cerca:** around
- **restaurante:** restaurant
- **dinheiro (em espécie):** cash
- **bem conhecido:** well known
- **de acordo:** according to
- **também:** also
- **antecedência:** in advance
- **gostosa:** delicious
- **pousadas:** lodging
- **café da manhã:** breakfast
- **energia:** energy
- **trilhas:** track
- **lindo:** pretty
- **pedras:** rocks
- **cores:** colors
- **mergulhar:** dive
- **almoçamos:** had lunch
- **pôr do sol:** sunset
- **espetáculo:** show
- **pesado:** heavy
- **bagagens:** luggage
- **lanches:** snacks
- **impressionante:** impressive
- **vista:** view
- **umidade:** humidity
- **quedas d'água:** waterfalls
- **praia:** beach
- **rio:** river
- **medo:** fear
- **assistir:** watch
- **preocupada:** worried
- **abelhas:** bees
- **perfumes:** perfumes
- **águas cristalinas:** clear waters
- **nascente:** wellspring
- **areia:** sand
- **incríveis:** incredible
- **fantásticas:** fantastic
- **transparência:** transparency
- **dormir:** sleep
- **fotos:** pictures
- **ao lado de:** alongside

Questions about the story

1. **Mateus conhece sobre a nova cidade a visitar:**

    a. tudo

    b. não conhece nada

    c. quase nada

    d. coisa alguma

2. **Qual foi a segunda pousada em que os amigos ficaram?**

    a. Pousada Vale da Lua

    b. Pousada Monte Videl

    c. Pousada Cachoeiras do Jalapão

    d. Pousada Águas do Jalapão

3. **Por que é preciso levar uma boa quantidade de dinheiro em espécie?**

    a. para não ser assaltado

    b. para evitar perder dinheiro

    c. porque alguns lugares não passam cartão

    d. porque alguns lugares passam cartão

4. **Como é o café da manhã das pousadas?**

    a. fraco e sem variedade

    b. excelente

    c. precisa encomendar antes

    d. o melhor que já provaram

5. **Como era a Lagoa do Japonês?**

    a. águas turvas e com muitas pedras

    b. refletia cores cristalinas

    c. águas cristalinas e cores belíssimas

    d. não recomendável para mergulho

Answers

1. C
2. B
3. C
4. B
5. C

CHAPTER TWO

NOUNS

Cadê a luz? – Where is the light?

Era uma **quinta-feira** e estávamos todos **ansiosos** pelo próximo **final de semana**, afinal era **véspera de Natal** e os preparativos já haviam começado.

Na minha **casa** somos em **quatro** pessoas, eu (Joana), meu **irmão** mais novo (Carlos) e meus pais (Joaquim e Selma), mas como toda **família** brasileira tínhamos muitos **parentes** e uma boa parte iria **celebrar** o Natal em nossa casa, pois na casa tem **piscina**, área externa grande, tudo encaminhado para fazer uma boa festa.

Logo, naquela mesma quinta-feira já começamos **arrumando** os **detalhes** para receber os parentes que vinham de **longe**, como a Tia Marta que estava vindo dos Estados Unidos. Nós sempre a tratamos muito bem; os **presentes** dela eram os melhores! Os tios José e Laura também chegariam na **sexta-feira**. Eles moravam na nossa cidade vizinha e eram excelentes tios, muito **amados**. No sábado chegariam meus **avós** paternos.

Logo pela **manhã** já fui requisitada pela minha mãe para ajeitar o quarto de meus avós, que precisava ficar no **andar** térreo, ter muitas toalhas e sem poeira.

- Joana, coloque todas essas **toalhas** no quarto em que seus avós sempre ficam, por favor. Ah, temos que **verificar** se está com muita poeira; acho que o aspirador resolve. Também devemos **encomendar** aqueles pães para o café da manhã e para **fazer** as rabanadas. – disse minha mãe.

- **Nossa**, quanta coisa!! Tomara que dê tudo certo! **Adoro** o Natal! Todos reunidos e felizes. Vai ter aquele mousse de **sobremesa**, também? – disse para minha mãe.

- **Claro**, minha filha! Teremos quatro sobremesas só para a ceia de Natal. Você poderá **escolher** qualquer uma ou até **repetir**! – disse minha mãe.

Como fiquei **feliz** com aquelas **palavras**. Sou uma verdadeira **apaixonada** por doces, principalmente as sobremesas de final de ano que são todas **muito boas**! Vou rapidamente colocar as toalhas no **quarto** e subo para verificar os outros quartos de **hóspedes**; afinal, teremos muitas visitas!

Observo que um dos quartos está sem **lâmpadas** e com muita poeira, dou um grito e chamo meu pai para verificar.

- Ei, senhor Joaquim, venha ver isso! – **grito** para meu pai.

O **coitado** subiu as escadas rápido demais, chegou no quarto tonto de tanto correr.

- O que foi minha filha, o que houve? Cadê a **barata**? – disse meu pai.

- Calma, pai! É somente para o senhor **averiguar** onde estão as lâmpadas deste quarto, pois sem elas fica difícil passar o **aspirador**, já que este será o quarto da tia Marta!!!!! – respondo para meu pai.

- Nossa, Joana! Não faça mais isso, achei que tinha **acontecido** algo. As lâmpadas estavam **queimadas**, tenho que comprar outras para repor, já estava ciente disso! Que susto, **menina**! – disse meu pai.

Nessa hora achei melhor sair de fininho para o **próximo** quarto: o de nossos tios. Este **acredito** que minha mãe já andou arrumando, pois está impecável, pronto para seus visitantes.

Olho pela **janela,** vejo meu pai e o Carlos saindo para **comprar** as lâmpadas e decido ir até a **cozinha** ajudar minha mãe com a comida do dia, que seria um almoço leve, e já preparar o **bolo** para o café da tarde.

Após a chegada dos dois, minha mãe decide **servir** o almoço. Eu estava com muita **fome**. Todos sentam à mesa. Eis que de repente a luz da rua acaba. Ficamos todos no escuro, mas como ainda era dia conseguimos almoçar sem problemas. A luz demorou cerca de duas horas para voltar, o que **atrasou** algumas tarefas da casa, mas nada grave.

Tia Marta estava prevista para chegar às cinco da tarde lá em casa, antes ela iria visitar uma **amiga** que seria a responsável por buscá-la no **aeroporto**. Próximo das cinco horas decido ir tomar banho e ficar à sua espera.

- Nossa, mãe! Daqui a pouco tia Marta está chegando, não vejo a hora de ouvir aquela **gargalhada**! – digo para minha mãe antes de subir para o banho.

- Como você gosta dessa sua tia! Também estou com saudade, afinal não podemos visitá-la com a **frequência** que gostaríamos. – disse minha mãe.

Lá de cima já escuto aquele grito da minha tia.

- SELMA, minha irmã! Que **saudades**, venha cá me dar um abraço! – grita tia Marta lá do portão.

- Minha irmã querida, como está você? Que linda que ficou com os **cabelos pintados**. – disse minha mãe.

Elas vão **conversando** até entrarem na casa e escuto tia Marta perguntando de mim e do meu irmão, **rapidamente** me visto e desço correndo as escadas; elas estavam na cozinha colocando o assunto em dia.

Novamente a luz acaba.

Tropeço no pé do sofá, dou o maior grito, todos veem me **ajudar**, mas está tudo bem, então **abraço** minha tia e matamos um pouco da saudade. Ficamos todos à mesa onde estava posto o lanche da tarde, com várias **velas** para suprir a falta de luz. Depois de duas horas a energia **retorna**.

Todos estávamos **cansados.** A tia Marta viajou bastante, eu e Carlos **exaustos** da arrumação e meus pais também pareciam um pouco abatidos. Cada um vai para o seu respectivo quarto e toda a casa fica em **silêncio**.

Na manhã seguinte, acordo com a **campainha** tocando. Eram meus avós e meus tios. Acabei não colocando o **despertador** para tocar e perdi o horário de acordar; eles chegaram mais cedo e de **surpresa**.

Escovo os dentes, lavo o rosto rapidamente e desço para recepcioná-los. Quanta **alegria** para uma casa só! Todos estamos muito felizes com a reunião. Meus avós estão radiantes e trouxeram doces de leite da **fazenda** e meus tios trouxeram outros doces e queijos para ceia.

O café da manhã foi **divertido** e cheio de **novidades.** Tia Marta estava pretendendo voltar a morar no **país**, meus avós iriam fazer um **cruzeiro** para idosos e meus tios finalmente decidiram adotar uma criança. Quanta novidade boa.

A energia novamente acaba. Dessa vez dura pouco, cerca de meia hora, e retorna. Meu pai chegou a ligar para a **companhia** da cidade, mas disseram que o problema já havia sido resolvido.

Começamos os **preparativos** para a ceia, como cozinhar os doces, os pratos principais, fazer as rabanadas e montar a mesa de comemoração que seria no jardim.

Quando **finalmente** acabamos os preparativos na cozinha e no jardim, todos fomos nos arrumar para realizar a ceia de Natal. Todos estávamos prontos para começar a ceia, meus avós pedem a **atenção** de todos, começam a fazer um discurso de **agradecimento**, e logo após a vovó parar de falar, adivinhe?

A energia acaba.

Ficamos todos naquela apreensão pelo retorno da energia, mas nada dela voltar. Nessa altura, meu **pai** junto com meu **tio** reúnem todas as velas e **lanternas** da casa. No final, a mesa estava iluminada como **antigamente**: à luz de velas; e alguns pontos com as lanternas.

Minha tia Marta como sempre **bem-humorada** faz **piada** da situação e todos nos sentamos na mesa, sem energia elétrica mesmo, e começamos a comemorar.

O meu Natal daquele ano foi **especial**, à **luz de velas,** e a energia fez pouca falta, pois eu estava **rodeada** de pessoas amadas.

Resumo da história

Joana e sua família estão se preparando para a noite de Natal. Todos os parentes virão para a sua casa, então é hora de preparar as comidas e bebidas, os quartos para os hóspedes e tudo mais o que precisar para que a ceia natalina seja um sucesso!

Summary of the story

Joan and her family are getting ready for Christmas Eve. All the relatives will come to their house, so it's time to prepare the food and drinks, the guest rooms and everything else needed to make the Christmas dinner a success!

Vocabulary

- **quinta-feira:** Thursday
- **ansiosos:** anxious
- **final de semana:** weekend
- **véspera de Natal:** Christmas Eve
- **casa:** house
- **quatro:** four
- **irmão:** brother
- **família:** family
- **parentes:** relatives
- **celebrar:** celebrate
- **piscina:** swimming pool
- **arrumando:** organizing
- **detalhes:** details
- **longe:** far
- **presentes:** gifts
- **sexta-feira:** Friday
- **amados:** loved
- **avós:** grandparents
- **manhã:** morning
- **andar:** floor
- **toalhas:** towels
- **verificar:** check
- **encomendar:** order
- **fazer:** to make
- **nossa:** gee!
- **adoro:** I love
- **sobremesa:** dessert
- **claro:** of course
- **escolher:** to choose
- **repetir:** to repeat
- **feliz:** happy
- **palavras:** words
- **apaixonada:** in love
- **muito boas:** very good
- **quarto:** bedroom
- **hóspedes:** guests
- **lâmpadas:** lamps
- **grito:** yell
- **coitado:** poor
- **barata:** cockroach
- **averiguar:** to check
- **aspirador:** vacuum cleaner
- **acontecido:** happened
- **queimadas:** burnt
- **menina:** girl
- **próximo:** next
- **acredito:** I believe
- **janela:** window
- **comprar:** buy
- **cozinha:** kitchen
- **bolo:** cake
- **servir:** serve
- **fome:** hunger

22

- **atrasou:** delayed
- **amiga:** friend
- **aeroporto:** airport
- **gargalhada:** laugh
- **frequência:** often
- **saudades:** to miss
- **cabelos pintados:** dyed hair
- **conversando:** talking
- **rapidamente:** quickly
- **novamente:** once again
- **ajudar:** help
- **abraço:** hug
- **velas:** candles
- **retorna:** comes back
- **cansados:** tired
- **exaustos:** exhausted
- **silêncio:** silent
- **campainha:** door bell
- **despertador:** alarm clock
- **surpresa:** surprise
- **escovo os dentes:** brush my teeth
- **alegria:** happines
- **fazenda:** farm
- **divertido:** funny
- **novidades:** news
- **país:** country
- **cruzeiro:** cruise
- **companhia:** company
- **preparativos:** preparations
- **finalmente:** finally
- **atenção:** attention
- **agradecimento:** thanks
- **pai:** father
- **tio:** uncle
- **lanternas:** lanterns
- **antigamente:** in the old days
- **bem-humorada:** good mood
- **piada:** joke
- **especial:** special
- **luz de velas:** candle light
- **rodeada:** surrounded

Questions about the story

1. Tia Marta sempre tinha:

   a. os melhores presentes

   b. os melhores doces

   c. os melhores queijos

   d. as melhores rabanadas

2. Quem precisava ficar no andar térreo?

   a. Tia Marta

   b. O avô e a avó

   c. Tio José e tia Laura

   d. Tio Joaquim e tia Selma

3. Quantas vezes a energia acaba ao longo da história?

   a. 2

   b. 3

   c. 4

   d. 5

4. Onde seria feita a comemoração?

   a. na sala de estar

   b. no quintal

   c. na sala de jantar

   d. no jardim

5. Como o problema da luz é solucionado pela família?

   a. com o retorno da luz pela companhia de energia

   b. com velas, lanternas e piadas

   c. com apreensão e lamento

   d. com um discurso de agradecimento

Answers

1. A
2. B
3. C
4. D
5. B

CHAPTER THREE

BASIC INSTRUCTIONS AND SIMPLE CONVERSATIONS

Férias Relâmpago – Quick Vacations

Como todo **início** de **verão** decido um **lugar** com muito **sol** e praia para visitar. O meu lugar preferido é a casa de minha tia, próximo à praia e com um clima maravilhoso. Então, resolvo **ligar** para saber se posso fazer uma **visita** prolongada. Ligo para **minha** tia:

- Alô, tia Sonia? É a Márcia, tudo bem?

- Oi, Márcia, tudo bem e com você? – **responde** Tia Sonia.

- Tudo bem também, está **chovendo** muito em Salvador? – **respondo** para minha tia.

- Não, **querida**. Aqui está com multo sol e **calor**; e em São Paulo? Está chovendo muito? – Disse minha tia **sobre** sua cidade.

- Está um pouco, mas **durante** a tarde faz muito calor também. A **diferença** é que não tenho praia próximo de mim. – Respondo para minha tia esperando que ela me **convide** para ir até sua cidade.

- Minha querida, por que não vem para cá? Você está de **férias** do trabalho?

- Estou de férias, sim. É uma **excelente** ideia, titia. Vou verificar as **passagens** e responder a senhora por **mensagem**. Pode ser?

- Sim, claro! **Aguardo** sua confirmação. – minha tia responde. – Mande um abraço para seu pai e um **beijo** a todos. Tenha um bom dia. – ela se **despede**.

- Beijos, tia! **Obrigada**. – Despeço-me e desligo o telefone.

Ligo o **computador** e compro as passagens para chegar até a cidade de minha tia, onde existem praias lindas, **gente** bonita e tenho vários amigos que moram por lá.

Pelo telefone envio mensagens confirmando minha ida para a cidade.

- Tia Sônia, já consegui **comprar** as passagens e chegarei em dois dias. **Resolvi** ficar quinze dias em sua casa, está tudo bem? – **escrevo** para minha tia.

- Sim, minha **sobrinha**. Estou à sua espera, envie o horário de chegada que seu **primo** irá buscá-la no aeroporto; afinal, você virá de avião? – responde minha tia.

- Irei de **avião** e vou chegar no voo das três e meia da tarde. Estarei esperando por ele no **saguão de desembarque**. Muito obrigada! – escrevo para minha tia.

- É um **prazer** recebê-la, irei agora mesmo arrumar o seu quarto. Até mais. -responde titia.

Com todas as passagens certas, resolvo ir até uma loja de **biquínis** de um **shopping** próximo da minha casa.

Chegando na loja avisto vários **modelos** de meu interesse, espero algum **funcionário** da loja para atendimento... Não demora muito e logo aparece uma senhora muito simpática para me atender.

- Boa tarde, senhorita. Posso ajudá-la? – disse a **vendedora**.

- Boa tarde, pode sim. Estou **interessada** em alguns modelos da loja. – respondo à moça.

- Que ótimo, posso pegar o tamanho certo para você. É possível **experimentar** a parte superior dos biquínis e as saias de praia. Qual seria o tamanho ideal? E como a senhorita se chama? – pergunta a vendedora.

- Meu tamanho é 42, gostaria de experimentar os modelos **azul**, **rosa**, **branco** e aqueles vestidos do canto esquerdo. Meu nome é Márcia, e o seu? – respondo para a vendedora.

- Está bem, vou buscar os tamanhos e modelos. Meu nome é Daniela, volto já. – disse a vendedora.

Daniela logo **retorna** com os modelos pedidos por mim e alguns extras caso eu goste e queira provar. Vou até o provador de roupas e experimento todas as peças. Acho que andei **comendo** muito hambúrguer, pois somente alguns modelos ficam bons.

- Então, senhorita Márcia, ficaram bons os modelos? Deseja provar mais alguns? – pergunta a vendedora.

- Daniela, estou **decidida** a levar esses três modelos, podemos levar até o **caixa**? – digo para a vendedora.

- Claro, fico feliz que tenha gostado. Foi um prazer, Márcia. – responde a vendedora da loja.

No final, decido comprar um biquíni azul e dois vestidos de praia para **sair** à noite ou ir em algum evento.

No dia seguinte vou até a **farmácia**, pois notei que não tinha mais **protetor solar** e creme hidratante. Esses itens são **essenciais** para quem vai à praia. Em uma caminhada de três minutos chego até a farmácia perto de minha casa.

Vou até o balcão de atendimento e pergunto se **alguém** poderia me ajudar. Logo um rapaz loiro se levanta da **cadeira** e me ajuda a esclarecer algumas dúvidas.

- Bom dia. Estou à procura de um bom protetor solar e hidratante para o corpo, devem ser bem resistentes. – Digo ao vendedor cujo crachá diz se chamar Elton.

- Claro, temos excelentes opções, seria para piscina, uso diário? – diz o vendedor.

- Seria para praia, estou indo daqui a dois dias. – respondo para o vendedor.

- **Entendi**, vou mostrar as **melhores** opções para a senhorita.

No fim, saio da farmácia com um protetor solar, um hidrante de corpo, uma loção pós sol, além de shampoo e condicionador em tamanho viagem. Que **prejuízo**!

Chego em casa e vou direto ao meu quarto **arrumar a mala**, não gosto de deixar para última hora. Tenho tanta roupa que fico até **indecisa** sobre o que levar. Após longas três horas consigo terminar de adequar minha mala para o destino praiano. Já fui tantas vezes que tenho muita coisa já pronta em casa.

No dia anterior à viagem vou até o mercado municipal comprar algum presente para titia. Lembro que ela adora algumas compotas que estão sempre a venda por lá. Aquele lugar é muito **grande** e legal. Compro três compotas para levar na viagem e alguns **queijos** para presentear. Eu almoço por ali mesmo e retorno para casa.

Ansiosa por minhas férias, estou muito feliz porque irei passar quinze dias na praia. Adoro a **época de calor**, fico bem melhor do que quando está frio na cidade.

Chega o grande dia. **Acordo** super disposta e organizo tudo para chegar com antecedência no aeroporto para que nenhum **imprevisto** atrapalhe minha viagem. O voo parte no horário previsto e demora cerca de duas horas e meia para chegar em Salvador. Logo ao sair do avião o ar já muda, posso sentir que estou próxima de uma praia.

Meu primo está à minha espera **conforme** combinamos e vamos direto ao encontro da titia. Ao chegar em sua casa já sou recebida com muito **carinho** e entrego os presentes; ela e meu primo adoraram.

Como pode imaginar, meus dias por lá foram **perfeitos**: muito sol, muita festa, muito descanso... dias excelentes! Já estou combinando o retorno em minhas próximas férias.

Resumo da história

Márcia está de férias e combina com sua tia para ficar em sua casa por alguns dias. Como a cidade para qual Márcia viajará é praiana, ela aproveita para arrumar a mala e comprar tudo o que precisa para a viagem de férias de última hora!

Summary of the story

Marcia is on vacation and agrees with her aunt to stay at her house for a few days. As the city to which Marcia will travel is by the sea, she takes the opportunity to pack everything she needs for the last-minute holiday trip!

Vocabulary

- **início:** beginning
- **verão:** summer
- **lugar:** place
- **sol:** sun
- **ligar:** call
- **visita:** visit
- **minha:** my
- **responde:** answers
- **chovendo:** raining
- **respondo:** reply
- **querida:** dear
- **calor:** warmth
- **sobre:** about
- **durante:** during
- **diferença:** difference
- **convide:** invites
- **férias:** vacations
- **excelente:** excellent
- **passagens:** tickets
- **mensagem:** message
- **aguardo:** wait
- **beijo:** kiss
- **despede:** says goodbye
- **obrigada:** thank you
- **computador:** computer
- **gente:** people
- **comprar:** to buy
- **resolvi:** decided

- **escrevo:** write
- **sobrinha:** niece
- **primo:** cousin
- **avião:** airplane
- **saguão de desembarque:** arrivals
- **prazer:** pleasure
- **biquínis:** bikinis
- **shopping:** mall
- **modelos:** models
- **funcionário:** staff
- **vendedora:** saleswoman
- **interessada:** interested
- **experimentar:** to try on
- **azul:** blue
- **rosa:** pink
- **branco:** white
- **retorna:** comes back
- **comendo:** eating
- **decidida:** decided
- **caixa:** cashier
- **sair:** go out
- **farmácia:** pharmacy
- **protetor solar:** sunscreen
- **essenciais:** essencials
- **alguém:** someone
- **cadeira:** chair
- **entendi:** understood

- **melhores:** best
- **prejuízo:** loss
- **arrumar a mala:** pack
- **indecisa:** unresolved
- **grande:** big
- **queijos:** cheese
- **época de calor:** summer time

- **acordo:** wake up
- **imprevisto:** unforseen
- **conforme:** as
- **carinho:** care
- **perfeitos:** perfect

Questions about the story

1. **Quais, segundo o texto, são as diferenças entre as cidades de Salvador e São Paulo?**

   a. nas duas chove muito

   b. nas duas faz muito calor

   c. em São Paulo não tem praia próxima

   d. em Salvador tem praia distante

2. **Márcia diz a sua tia que vai verificar as passagens e retorna por:**

   a. ligação

   b. mensagem

   c. Skype

   d. convite

3. **Em que lugar Márcia vai esperar pelo primo?**

   a. no saguão do embarque

   b. no saguão do aeroporto

   c. no saguão do desembarque

   d. no saguão, ao longo do ponto de taxi

4. **Quais cores de biquínis Márcia gostaria experimentar?**

   a. azul, rosa e branco

   b. amarelo, rosa e preto

   c. azul, preto e amarelo

   d. preto, azul e rosa

5. **Na farmácia, por que Márcia teve um prejuízo?**

   a. porque os produtos estavam caros

   b. porque não esperava gastar pouco

   c. porque não comprou tudo o que precisava

   d. porque levou mais coisas do que o esperado

Answers

1. C
2. B
3. C
4. A
5. D

CHAPTER FOUR

PRONOUNS

Onde está meu relógio? – Where is my watch?

Eu acordo **geralmente** às oito da manhã, coloco a **cafeteira** para funcionar enquanto **tomo banho** e escolho a **roupa** para ir trabalhar. Retorno à cozinha e o café já está a minha espera, assim como o preparo breve de uma **torrada** com **manteiga**.

Após o **desjejum**, visto a roupa e termino de me arrumar em menos de dez minutos. No fim estou pronta quinze minutos antes das nove horas, tempo **suficiente** para chegar ao meu trabalho que é ao lado de minha casa.

Tudo **cronometrado** e observado de perto com meu relógio, um clássico Cartier **herdado** de minha mãe, prateado com realces em verde, simples, porém **extremamente** pontual e eficaz. Ela resolveu me presentear em meu aniversário de dezoito anos, isso já tem algum tempo, mas o **relógio** se tornou um companheiro ao longo de muitas temporadas. Fico muito feliz em poder usar algo que um dia foi dela.

Eu sou **estilista**, tenho meu próprio ateliê em Paris já faz vinte e dois anos, **costumo** receber minhas clientes com hora marcada, sou especialista em alta costura. Comigo, as moças da alta sociedade encontram seus finos tecidos, modernos cortes e costura exemplares.

Adoro **pontualidade** e em meu ateliê nós sempre buscamos levar o horário com muita seriedade. Apenas quatro pessoas trabalham **diariamente** comigo: duas **costureiras** escolhidas com muita precisão, uma responsável pela **limpeza,** e a **recepcionista** e auxiliar geral. Nós somos um time e tanto, temos agenda cheia pelos próximos seis meses e trabalhamos arduamente.

Comigo o **compromisso** é levado com muita destreza. Hoje consigo ter algumas folgas por ano de no máximo vinte dias; costumo viajar para os **desfiles** de alta costura pelo mundo; adoro participar e **renovar** as ideias. Daqui a uma semana estarei embarcando para Milão onde o primeiro evento de alta costura do ano acontece.

Os preparativos já começam com o preparo da mala: tenho que estar **deslumbrante** todos os dias, e como temos uma intervalo grande entre o **cliente** de duas da tarde e o de seis horas, decido experimentar algumas **confecções** que eu mesma **desenhei,** e com a ajuda de minhas costureiras conseguimos tornar realidade, dois vestidos e um blazer que ficam esplêndidos.

- Parabéns, meninas, nós conseguimos um ótimo resultado. Conosco, o trabalho é sempre prazeroso, não é mesmo? Eles iram adorar nossas **criações**, já prevejo uma enxurrada de novas clientes. O que acham? – **Parabenizo** e pergunto às costureiras.

- Sim, madame! A senhora está **magnífica** com os vestidos e o blazer deu o toque final que as peças precisavam. Tu estás linda. – responde Monique (minha costureira mais antiga).

- **Com certeza**, nós formamos uma excelente equipe. Madame Julie, podíamos fazer o terceiro vestido, acredito que temos tempo para fazê-lo. O que acha? – responde Anna (a mais nova costureira).

- Se acham que tem **condições** de fazer, vamos ao trabalho! – respondo às meninas.

Naquele dia fico muito feliz e retorno para casa cansada, mas com um **sentimento** de realização muito bom.

No dia seguinte toda a rotina se repete, e vai sendo assim até o **penúltimo** dia que antecede a viagem quando o terceiro vestido fica pronto e vou ao **ateliê** fazer a prova antes de eu terminar os últimos detalhes da viagem. Provo o vestido que é o mais bonito de todos, um azul escuro deslumbrante, **brilhoso** e muito adequado ao meu manequim. Eu não consigo acreditar que estava vestindo algo tão bonito.

Nós começamos a admirar no **espelho** enorme que eu possuo na loja o quão bonito era aquele **vestido**. Resolvo tirar várias fotos e peço para que todas apareçam, afinal é um trabalho em equipe. Senhorita Alice (recepcionista) fica tímida, mas insisto para que apareça nas fotos, enquanto Dona Lina fica toda emocionada por ter sido chamada. O dia **termina** muito bem, tudo está perfeitamente encaminhado.

- Garanto-lhes que farei muito **sucesso** nos desfiles com este vestido, nosso ateliê vai ficar mais famoso e todas nós seremos recompensadas, ouviram meninas? – digo toda feliz para minhas funcionárias.

Volto para casa, ajusto os últimos **detalhes** e vou dormir mais cedo, pois estava cansada. Na manhã seguinte acordo com o telefone **tocando** às onze da manhã, **inacreditável**, eu nunca acordara tão tarde assim. Quando atendo era somente a moça do telemarketing; ainda levantei para atender isso.

O voo estava marcado para as sete da noite e o **caminho** da minha casa até o aeroporto durava cerca de quarenta minutos, ou seja, tinha que sair de casa com antecedência. Após acordar tarde, vou até a **cozinha** e preparo um café reforçado para conseguir mais energia para o dia.

Estava com um **pressentimento** ruim, mas decido ignorar. Levo o dia normalmente, quando estou lendo o jornal e de repente recebo outro telefonema: era a companhia de táxi perguntando se o motorista poderia sair para me buscar daqui a duas horas. Como assim, duas horas? Como o tempo passou tão depressa?

Vou ao **banheiro** e começo a tomar um banho rapidamente. Ao começar a fechar minhas malas num susto me dou conta: onde está o meu relógio?

Entro em choque, não consigo raciocinar, não faço ideia de onde ele está. **Procuro** na casa toda e nada. Eu começo a entrar em desespero. Nego-me a viajar sem o meu precioso relógio.

Ligo para o ateliê na esperança de ter deixado por lá, mas ninguém atende, pois, as meninas também não iriam trabalhar naquele dia. Resolvo ir até lá rapidamente, e como o dia não estava favorável, o **sapato** que calçava machucava muito o pé (não lembrava desse detalhe) e chego com muita dificuldade.

Começo pela entrada e também não avisto nada, nem sinal do relógio. De repente a porta se abre, a Dona Lina tinha chegado para limpar o ateliê, ela gostava de trocar as segundas-feiras pelo sábado à tarde (menos movimentado). Faço uma rápida **explicação,** e começamos a busca pelo relógio sem sucesso. Quando decido retornar para casa, escuto um grito de dentro do provador.

- Madame, madame!!! Achei! Não é este o seu relógio? – grita Dona Lina.

- Sim, sim, sim! Onde o achou? – pergunto.

- Logo ali no fundo daquele tapete. Deve ter caído ontem na prova do vestido azul! – responde Lina.

Agradeço muito a ajuda de Dona Lina e vou correndo para casa. Por **sorte** tinha sapatos mais confortáveis no ateliê.

Ao chegar à portaria do meu prédio, o taxista já está a minha espera e, como num passe de **mágica**, ao colocar o relógio em meu pulso tudo começa a se encaixar em seu devido tempo. Chego com folga no aeroporto, o **voo** está no horário, e prossigo com minha viagem.

Pode parecer superstição, mas, o meu relógio, esse eu não perco nunca mais!

Resumo da história

Uma estilista famosa por seu atelier e costura impecáveis está procurando um bem muito preciso para si: um relógio que ganhara de sua mãe pouco antes dos vinte anos de idade. Sem o seu relógio, a estilista não consegue seguir seus hábitos adequadamente, pois é muito pontual.

Summary of the story

A fashion designer famous for her impeccable atelier and sewing is looking for a very precious item to her, a watch she had earned from her mother just before she was twenty. Without her watch, the designer cannot follow her habits properly because she is very punctual.

Vocabulary

- **geralmente:** usually
- **cafeteira:** coffee machine
- **tomo banho:** I take a shower
- **roupa:** clothes
- **torrada:** toast
- **manteiga:** butter
- **desjejum:** breakfast
- **suficiente:** enough
- **cronometrado:** timed
- **herdado:** inherited
- **extremamente:** extremely
- **relógio:** watch
- **estilista:** stylist / fashion designer
- **costumo:** be used to – I am used to
- **pontualidade:** punctuality
- **diariamente:** daily
- **costureiras:** dressmakers
- **limpeza:** cleaning
- **recepcionista:** receptionist
- **compromisso:** appointment
- **desfiles:** fashion show - parades
- **renovar:** to renew
- **deslumbrante:** gorgeous
- **cliente:** client
- **confecções:** clothing
- **desenhei:** designed
- **criações:** creations
- **parabenizo:** congratulate
- **magnífica:** magnificent
- **com certeza:** for sure
- **condições:** conditions
- **sentimento:** feelings
- **ateliê:** studio
- **brilhoso:** shiny
- **espelho:** mirror
- **vestido:** dress
- **termina:** ends
- **sucesso:** success
- **detalhes:** details
- **tocando:** ringing
- **inacreditável:** unbelievable
- **caminho:** way
- **cozinha:** kitchen
- **pressentimento:** feeling
- **banheiro:** bathroom
- **procuro:** (I) search
- **sapato:** shoe
- **explicação:** explanation
- **sorte:** luck
- **mágica:** magic
- **voo:** flight

Questions about the story

1. **Todos os dias ao acordar precisamente às oito da manhã, a estilista:**

   a. prepara uma torrada, toma banho, escolhe a roupa e prepara o café

   b. escolhe a roupa, prepara o café, toma banho e prepara uma torrada

   c. prepara o café, escolhe a roupa, toma banho e prepara uma torrada

   d. prepara o café, toma banho, escolhe a roupa e prepara uma torrada

2. **O relógio da estilista era:**

   a. clássico, prateado com realces em preto

   b. um clássico Cartier herdado de sua tia

   c. extremamente pontual e ineficaz

   d. um presente herdado de sua mãe

3. **Depois de ajustar os últimos detalhes, a estilista dorme e acorda:**

   a. atrasada, às 9h da manhã

   b. adiantada às 10h da manhã

   c. atrasada, às 10h da manhã

   d. atrasada, às 11h da manhã

4. **A estilista entra em desespero, pois:**

   a. se recusa a viajar com o relógio

   b. se nega a viajar com o relógio

   c. se nega a procurar o relógio

   d. se recusa a viajar sem o relógio

5. A estilista, ao chegar na portaria do prédio:

   a. encontra o taxista a sua espera

   b. encontra o manobrista a sua espera

   c. encontra a diarista a sua espera

   d. encontra o taxista reclamando da espera

Answers

1. D
2. D
3. D
4. D
5. A

CHAPTER FIVE

EXPRESSIONS AND FIGURATIVE LANGUAGE

Reunião mensal do grupo do bolinha – Monthly Guys Group Meeting

Era uma sexta-feira, dia **marcado** para o encontro do nosso **grupo** de amigos. Somos muito enrolados, no entanto, o encontro sempre **tarda** mas não falha. Escolhemos o **bar** de sempre, o Pinguim. Marcamos às dez horas da noite, horário perfeito para todos.

O grupo tinha cinco **pessoas**, uma mais **desvairada** que a outra, que mesmo com **compromissos** durante o dia e andando na linha, à noite podíamos chutar o balde. Nos **encontramos** Danilo (Dandan), Rafael (enrolado), Thiago (nervosinho), Otávio (chefinho) e Eu (Jorge),

Mais cedo, Dandan havia me **ligado. Sinceramente** achei que o encontro tinha ido pelo cano, mas era **somente** para perguntar se eu precisaria de **carona**. Aceitei, pois queria beber um pouco, andava muito **estressado** e precisava extravasar.

- Opa, Danilo, aceito sua carona, você passa aqui em casa que horas? Estou quase enfiando o pé na jaca **comendo** batata frita com meu filho. – respondi para Dandan.

- Jorginho, estou passando aí daqui a meia hora, vá se arrumar! – disse Danilo.

Vou então **trocar de roupa** e avisar minha **esposa** que estou indo no encontro de amigos, o famoso mensalão. Ela me deu uma **olhada** traiçoeira, achei que fosse brigar comigo, mas somente deu um belo grito:

- Cuidado, você pode estar pisando em ovos com esse seu mensalão! – grita minha esposa lá do **quintal**.

- O que você quis dizer com isso? É somente um encontro **inofensivo**, daqui a pouco estou de volta em casa, fique **tranquila**, meu amor! – respondo para ela.

Minha esposa sempre foi um pouco **ciumenta**, mas ela também tinha os encontros dela com suas amigas. As vezes esses encontros eram em nossa casa, macacos me mordam! Na hora decido verificar se o pessoal não gostaria de ir até a minha casa, seria muito divertido e **cômodo** para todos.

Mando mensagem em nosso grupo na internet.

- Fala, meus amigos, suave na nave? Que tal **realizar** nosso encontro em minha **residência**? Aqui podemos ficar mais à vontade e se quiserem podem trazer seus filhos e esposas. Podemos jogar baralho, **jogar conversa fora** e ficar até o dia raiar. O que acham? – pergunto a todos.

- Jorginho, eu estou correndo da minha esposa como o diabo foge da cruz, **prefiro** que seja no bar mesmo, ela está muito brava, pois comprei mais um acessório para o carro, um pouco caro, coisa pouca, sabe? – responde o Rafa.

- Cara, eu topo. Moro perto da sua casa! Vamos nessa! – responde o chefinho.

- Jorge! Oh Jorge! VAMOS AO BAR! Sair de casa, ver gente nova, estou **solteiro**, me ajuda rapaz! – responde o nervosinho.

- Jorginho, estou passando em frente à sua casa, vamos logo para o bar! – responde Danilo.

Meus **planos** foram por água abaixo. Me arrumo **correndo** e fico à espera de Danilo que logo chega. Saio de casa. Danilo adora tanto se exibir que até suspeitei quando ofereceu carona. Acabara de comprar um carro novo; era realmente **espetacular,** mas deve ter custado um **rim**.

- Jorginho, esse carro é show! Melhor aquisição dos últimos tempos, depois deixo você **dar uma voltinha**. – comenta Dandan.

- Estou fora! Hoje vou **beber**, logo não posso **dirigir**! Mas realmente seu carro é show! Parabéns, Dandan.

Somos os primeiros do grupo a chegar no Pinguim, já peço minha **cerveja** estupidamente gelada para o garçom.

- Ei, moço, traz aquela que você guardou especialmente para o final da noite? – peço ao garçom.

- Claro, já trago. – o garçom responde.

- Rapaz, traga um drink não alcoólico, hoje sou o motorista da vez. – pede Danilo.

- Ihh, ficou para escanteio? Trago sim, aqui temos um drink que o senhor nem vai sentir falta do álcool de tão bom que é. – responde o garçom.

Olho para Danilo e decido comentar algo com ele.

- Cara, vou abrir o jogo contigo. – digo para Dandan.

- Vai revelar que **trapaceou** naquele jogo da semana passada? – fala Dandan morrendo de rir.

- Não! Não! – digo para Danilo rindo – Eu ia comentar contigo que achava que esse encontro nem ia realmente acontecer, sabe? Mas vejo que somos um grupo muito unido. As vezes comento com o pessoal do **trabalho** e poucos têm amigos de longa data igual a nós. E muito bacana, entende?

- Claro, no meu trabalho também falam a mesma coisa, quando vocês comentam em minhas fotos com aquelas piadas internas o pessoal fica doido para saber nossas histórias. Foram muitas. – responde Dandan.

Nesse período chega o Thiago (nervosinho), que como sempre já chega **reclamando** de alguma coisa que aconteceu no caminho.

- Carambolas! O rapaz do táxi estava virando a **esquina** para estacionar aqui e de repente um cara em uma **bicicleta** entra do nada na frente do veículo, que homem louco! Deu sorte que o motorista parou a tempo de evitar um acidente. Eu não dou sorte com taxista!! Não me leve a mal pessoal, precisava **desabafar**! – Thiago chega esbaforido.

- Garçom, traz uma água que passarinho não bebe! – Thiago grita para o garçom. – Então, como estão vocês dois? – ele pergunta para nós que no momento estamos **morrendo de rir** do nervosinho.

- Tudo certo, meu jovem! – respondo para Thiago.

- E você, como está? Além de não dar sorte com os **taxistas**? – Danilo pergunta para ele.

Na mesma hora chegam juntos o Rafa e o Otávio. Todos se cumprimentam e de repente estamos dando boas risadas das histórias que cada um tem para contar.

- Ei, Jorginho, pare de andar nas **nuvens**! Presta atenção na conversa. – O chefinho fala para mim.

Realmente eu estava no mundo da lua. Estava pensando na sorte de ter bons e únicos amigos para compartilhar a vida, poucos tem esse privilégio.

- Opa, desculpe, desculpe! Já estou de volta! Vamos pedir uns petiscos? Estou com fome. – pergunto ao pessoal.

- Você sempre está com fome, Jorginho. – comenta o Rafa.

- É verdade, olha o **tamanho** da minha barriga! Preciso emagrecer! Você podia me dar algumas dicas já que está indo bem como personal trainer. – respondo para o Rafa.

- Posso e vou! Se começar a treinar comigo, rapidinho você emagrece! – retruca Rafa.

De repente, todos nós já havíamos combinando de criar um grupo de corrida, pois estávamos todos acima do peso, menos o Rafa.

Então, será que conseguiríamos arcar com mais esse compromisso? Não sei, só sei que a conversa terminou quando o bar fechou. Bem que eu falei para fazermos o encontro lá na minha toca!!

Resumo da história

Um grupo de amigos faz de tudo para continuarem os encontros mensais, para colocar os assuntos em dia e manter a amizade de anos. O difícil é fugir dos outros compromissos para arrumar um horário em que todos possam se encontrar, mas eles vão insistindo e a amizade continua.

Summary of the story

A group of friends do everything they can to continue their monthly meetings to keep up with their catch up and maintain a friendship that has existed for years. The difficult thing is to get away from the other commitments to arrange a time when everyone can meet; but they insist and their friendship continues.

Vocabulary

- **marcado:** scheduled
- **grupo:** group
- **tarde:** delays
- **bar:** bar
- **pessoas:** people
- **desvairada:** crazy
- **compromisso:** appointment
- **encontramos:** meet
- **ligado:** called
- **sinceramente:** honestly
- **somente:** only
- **carona:** ride
- **estressado:** stressed
- **comendo:** eating
- **trocar de roupa:** get changed
- **esposa:** wife
- **olhada:** look
- **quintal:** yard
- **inofensivo:** harmless
- **tranquila:** calm
- **ciumenta:** jealous
- **cômodo:** comfortable
- **realizar:** to make
- **residência:** house

- **jogar conversa fora:** small talk
- **prefiro:** prefer
- **solteiro:** single
- **planos:** plans
- **correndo:** running
- **espetacular:** spetacular
- **rim:** kidney
- **dar uma voltinha:** go for a ride
- **beber:** to drink
- **dirigir:** to drive
- **cerveja:** beer
- **trapaceou:** cheated
- **trabalho:** work
- **reclamando:** complaining
- **esquina:** corner
- **bicicleta:** bike
- **desabafar:** unburden
- **morrendo de rir:** laughing out loud
- **taxista:** cab driver
- **nuvens:** clouds
- **tamanho:** size
- **de repente:** suddenly

Questions about the story

1. **O trecho,"o encontro tarda, mas não falha" significa:**
   a. que o encontro não acontece
   b. que o encontro acontece
   c. ninguém vai ao encontro
   d. o encontro é antecipado

2. **No texto, a expressão "andar na linha" significa:**
   a. fazer tudo certo
   b. fazer tudo errado
   c. se comportar de forma estranha
   d. andar em cima de uma linha branca

3. **Jorge acha que o carro de Dandan "deve ter custado um rim", o que significa:**
   a. que o carro era feio
   b. que o carro era marrom
   c. que o carro era caro
   d. que o carro não compensava

4. **Ao pedir ao garçom que traga uma "água que passarinho não bebe", Thiago quis dizer:**
   a. para trazer suco de frutas
   b. para não trazer água
   c. para trazer bebida alcóolica
   d. para trazer bebida sem álcool

5. **O bar fechou antes dos amigos conseguirem conversar sobre tudo. O que Jorge quis dizer com "bem que eu falei para fazer o encontro lá na minha toca"?**
   a. que deveriam ter feito o encontro na casa dele

b. que não deveriam ter feito o encontro
c. que deveriam ter feito o encontro em uma toca
d. que deveriam ter feito o encontro em uma festa

Answers

1. B
2. A
3. C
4. D
5. A

CHAPTER SIX

NUMBERS

Uma viagem com amigos em pleno fim de ano – A trip with friends at the very end of the year

Nessa **época** de final de ano as **lembranças** sempre aparecem e com elas **relembramos** histórias **engraçadas** que nos trazem um **conforto** emocional imenso. Hoje com meus trinta anos bem vividos e a **carreira** de **engenharia** em ascensão, me pego recordando da época de **faculdade**, onde vivi histórias muito engraçadas, mas que no fundo sempre nos trazem algum **aprendizado**. Vou contar uma delas aqui de quando estava morando numa **pensão** junto com outros estudantes que considero até hoje **verdadeiros amigos**.

Era época de provas finais na universidade e todos estavam com a cabeça a mil por hora tentando **recuperar** o conteúdo atrasado e conseguir **notas** suficientes nas **disciplinas** – está certo que em algumas, como a de cálculo, o **desafio** era grande.

Esse **período** teve uma duração de duas semanas. Ao **final,** já estávamos em plena semana de Natal. O último **semestre** letivo daquele ano foi de arrasar, muito puxado e necessitava de uma grande carga horária de estudos e dezenas de trabalhos finais para **terminar**.

Naquele tempo éramos um grupo de sete amigos **inseparáveis** (Daniel, Cris, Pietro, João, Paulinho, Renato, e eu, Rafael), com três coisas em comum: o curso de engenharia, morarmos na mesma pensão e a **distância** de casa. Em termos de **personalidade** éramos muito diferentes, sempre acontecia alguma **confusão**, mas no final nos entendíamos bem; era como se tivéssemos um tipo de equilíbrio. Bom, vamos à história daquele fim de ano de 2007.

Estava na sala de estudos quando Paulinho de repente me perguntou:

- Rafa, após as **provas** você vai passar o Natal por aqui?

- Paulinho, estou achando que ficarei por aqui mesmo, o **dinheiro** está pouco e a passagem para minha cidade está custando mais de mil reais!

- Nossa cara, estou com o mesmo problema, o que aconteceu com o preço das passagens?

- Pois é, nem me fale, vou ficar sem as rabanadas da minha mãe!!

Naquela época, estávamos enfrentando uma **greve** de rodoviários e os caminhões-tanque com **combustíveis** de aviação não conseguiam chegar aos aeroportos e com a gasolina havia o mesmo problema, portanto, as companhias que ainda conseguiam **operar** estavam cobrando caro demais!! Passagens de avião que antes custavam duzentos reais estavam na faixa de oitocentos reais, um acréscimo enorme, e ir de **ônibus** também custava caro, além disso, o tempo entre o término das provas e as festas era curto e para chegar rápido ao nosso **destino**, era sempre mais eficaz ir de avião.

No mesmo dia outros três amigos também falaram que passariam as festas de final do ano na pensão. Como éramos, na época, **jovens** aventureiros, começamos a pensar no que faríamos se ficássemos ali mesmo na cidade. Após algumas **pesquisas** descobrimos que estaríamos a ver navios naquela cidade, pois a maioria das pessoas iria viajar de volta para casa, já que ali era uma **cidade universitária** e poucos estudantes realmente tinham família naquele lugar.

O Cris era o cara mais festivo e animado do grupo e também não conseguiria voltar para casa naquele ano. De repente, ele descobriu por meio de amigos sobre uma **excursão** em promoção para um lugar paradisíaco que fica a uns 200 km de onde morávamos. Pronto, começou todo o **planejamento** para tentar levar todo mundo para essa viagem.

Mas ainda faltava convencer mais dois **companheiros** de que essa viagem seria **fantástica**. Em meio às sessões de estudos, Paulinho procurava dezenas de imagens das **cachoeiras** do local no computador e mostrava para todos. Cris, na tentativa de animar os que ainda estavam indecisos, falava ao telefone bem alto que já estava tudo combinado e discutia sobre as festas, cachoeiras, bares. Com isso, Pietro veio conversar comigo sobre essa viagem.

- Rafa, estou pensando nas provas que tenho que fazer, mas essa viagem não sai da minha cabeça. Será que vai valer a pena? Realmente está muito barato natal e ano novo por novecentos reais. Você vai? – Perguntou Pietro.

- Claro que vou!! Não posso perder e você também não! Vamos amigo, vai ser bom demais!! – Respondi para Pietro.

Após algumas provas feitas com sucesso e muita conversa com os **pais** dele, Pietro decide ir conosco, afinal sua cidade também estava com passagens caras e seus pais decidiram que iriam para a casa de seus avós passar as festas de final de ano. Por isso, iria cumprir sua **missão** nessa viagem fantástica. Mas ainda tinha um deles que não se decidira: o João. Pense num rapaz **tímido** que só pensa em estudar, estudar e estudar. Já estávamos nos últimos dias de prova e a **promoção** também não iria durar para sempre.

O Cris, o mais popular da turma, começou a pensar em como levar o João para essa viagem que tinha que ter os sete reunidos para ser **memorável**. Apesar de seu jeito fechado e tímido, sabíamos que João tinha uma **queda** pela Renatinha que cursava engenharia conosco. Os dois eram tímidos e não conseguiam se encontrar. Foi pensando nela que o Cris correu atrás de seu contato e adivinha só? Renatinha também iria na viagem com suas amigas de pensão. Era **impressionante** como tudo se encaixava.

Quando contamos a notícia para João, logo o rapaz se animou. Ele estava realmente **apaixonado** pela moça e até roupas novas comprou para viagem. Ele queria emagrecer também, mas já estava em cima da hora.

Os "sete mosqueteiros" iriam passar as festas de final de ano juntos, num dos lugares mais bonitos da redondeza. O destino com certeza ajudou. Num primeiro momento estávamos todos tristes porque não iríamos rever nossas famílias, porém há sempre **o lado bom das coisas.** Não é todo dia que se viaja com seus **melhores amigos**, ainda mais por sermos sete era muito difícil dar certo de viajar com todos, entre datas, recursos, etc.

O dia anterior à viagem chegou, e com ele toda aquela confusão em arrumar malas, decidir quais comidas e **bebidas** levar, confirmar tudo e verificar as tais temidas notas das provas e trabalhos. Confesso que estava mais **nervoso** com as notas do que com os detalhes da viagem, mas no fim deu tudo certo. O Renato, como sempre, gabaritando todas as provas e competindo com João pelos melhores resultados, o Cris meio descrente com a faculdade e o restante ficou naquela zona de conforto.

No **dia seguinte** partimos para o destino e foi uma das viagens mais fantásticas que já fiz. Como era divertido estar no ônibus com todo aquele grupo. No percurso até a pousada me pegava admirando como é bom ter amigos, ter com quem rir de besteiras, piadas, contar histórias, **contar** coisas inimagináveis, fazer planos mirabolantes para o futuro. Fiquei até **emocionado** com aquele sentimento todo dentro de mim e, é claro, fui caçoado pelos amigos que me viram daquele jeito, mas, no fim, passei férias emocionantes ao lado desses **caras**!!! Quem tem amigos tem tudo!

Resumo da história

Quem nunca passou por situações que valem a pena contar? Rafael conta sobre a história de sua juventude que aconteceu quando ainda era estudante de engenharia e morava em uma pensão com seus amigos.

Summary of the story

Who has never had situations that are worth telling? Rafael tells the story of his youth that happened when he was still an engineering student and lived in a boarding house with his friends.

Vocabulary

- **época:** time
- **lembranças:** memories
- **relembramos:** remembered
- **engraçadas:** funny
- **conforto:** confort
- **carreira:** career
- **engenharia:** engineering
- **faculdade:** university
- **aprendizado:** learning
- **pensão:** pension
- **verdadeiros amigos:** true friends
- **recuperar:** to recover
- **notas:** grades
- **disciplinas:** subjects
- **desafio:** challenge
- **período:** period
- **final:** end
- **semestre:** semester
- **terminar:** to finish
- **inseparáveis:** inseparable
- **personalidade:** personality
- **confusão:** confusion
- **provas:** tests
- **dinheiro:** money
- **greve:** stroke
- **combustíveis:** fuel
- **operar:** to work
- **ônibus:** bus
- **destino:** destination
- **jovens:** young
- **pesquisas:** researches
- **cidade universitária:** university city
- **excursão:** tour
- **planejamento:** planning
- **companheiros:** companions
- **fantástica:** fantastic
- **cachoeiras:** waterfalls
- **pais:** parents
- **missão:** mission
- **tímido:** shy
- **promoção:** promotion
- **memorável:** memorable
- **queda:** crush
- **impressionante:** impressive
- **apaixonado:** in love
- **lago:** lake
- **lado bom das coisas:** the bright side of things
- **melhores amigos:** best friends

- **bebidas:** beverages
- **nervoso:** nervous
- **dia seguinte:** following day
- **contar:** to tell
- **emocionado:** affected
- **caras:** dudes

Questions about the story

1. **Quantos amigos Rafael tinha?**

    a. 5

    b. 9

    c. 6

    d. 4

2. **Quais destes 3 eram seus amigos?**

    a. Daniel, Marcos, Renato.

    b. Daniel, Cris, Pietro.

    c. João, Paulão e André.

    d. Paulo, Marcos e Frederico.

3. **Quantos anos tem Rafael atualmente?**

    a. quarenta e cinco

    b. trinta e dois

    c. quarenta

    d. trinta

4. **Quanto custou a viagem para passar o natal e o ano novo?**

    a. duzentos reais.

    b. novecentos reais.

    c. quatrocentos reais.

    d. mil reais.

    e. trezentos reais.

5. **Quem competia pelos melhores resultados nos exames?**

    a. Renato e João.

    b. Paulinho e Pietro.

    c. Daniel e Frederico.

    d. Rafael e Paulão.

Answers

1. C
2. B
3. D
4. B
5. A

CHAPTER SEVEN

ADJETIVES

O trem para Budapeste - The train to Budapest

Era um dia de muito calor e com o **céu** aberto no qual duas pessoas teriam suas vidas **cruzadas** para sempre.

Roberto estava **atrasado** para chegar até a Estação Luz **em tempo** de pegar o **trem** para casa de seus pais em Budapeste. Sua casa ficava a duas quadras da estação mas, como bom **soldado,** queria deixar todo o **apartamento** perfeitamente seguro e arrumado, e acabou se atrasando com a janela da cozinha que havia emperrada.

Do outro lado da cidade estava Carla, uma moça muito **bonita**, com **cabelos castanhos claros** e pele morena, que pegaria o mesmo trem e também estava atrasada, mas como a pontualidade não era seu ponto forte, acabou demorando muito no **banho** e atrasou todo o **cronograma**.

Os dois pegaram táxis diferentes, embora praticamente no mesmo momento, percorreram distâncias parecidas e chegaram à estação faltando alguns minutos para o **embarque**.

Roberto comprou passagem na **primeira classe** e sentou na poltrona 1. Precavido como era já havia aproveitado uma promoção e adquirido seu bilhete meses antes da viagem.

Carla comprou passagem na segunda classe para economizar e gastar na viagem, mas quando chegou em seu assento ele já estava ocupado por um senhor. Para resolver Carla tentou **conversar** com o mesmo.

- Boa tarde, Senhor. Desculpe, mas acredito que o senhor está **sentado** em meu lugar.

- Boa tarde, minha jovem. Tem certeza? No meu bilhete marca esta poltrona. – O senhor retirou de seu bolso o **bilhete** e mostrou pra Carla.

- Minha nossa, como podem vender dois bilhetes para a mesma poltrona? – Carla correu até o **funcionário** mais próximo.

Questionada pelo funcionário da companhia que estava uniformizado e prontamente ao dispor dos **passageiros** sobre o bilhete que havia comprado, ela o retira de sua carteira e mostra para o jovem que tenta **resolver** a situação. Ao analisar o bilhete, o funcionário muito simpático tenta conversar com Carla, pois ele já havia encontrado o **defeito**: o bilhete que ela contestava era para uma viagem três dias posteriores do dia atual.

Muito **envergonhada** ela tenta conversar sobre a **possibilidade** de comprar uma passagem para aquela data.

- Poderia comprar uma para a viagem de **hoje**, qualquer uma, já estou **acostumada** com as minhas maluquices, sou muito atrapalhada, que cabeça a minha! Agora tenho familiares me esperando em Budapeste, que confusão... – e Carla segue tentando **argumentar** e **adquirir** uma nova passagem, mesmo sabendo que está atrasando a partida do trem.

Percebendo a impaciência de alguns passageiros que começam a reclamar com os funcionários dentro do trem, o responsável **propõe** para a moça que adquira uma mudança para a primeira classe, pois lá estaria o único lugar disponível do trem.

Muito **aborrecida** por tamanha trapalhada, Carla aceita **comprar** uma passagem que no final saiu muito mais cara do que o esperado. Ao chegar na primeira classe, sua poltrona está a sua espera, sendo esta a de número três.

Roberto, ao avistar o funcionário da companhia, **gesticula** sobre o atraso na partida do trem.

- Meu jovem trabalhador, o trem irá partir que horas? Já chegaremos atrasados no destino final, tenho compromissos marcados para hoje!! Já me encontro impaciente e nervoso pelo atraso.

- Desculpe, senhor. Houve um imprevisto, mas já foi solucionado. – O funcionário **acomoda** Carla em seu assento neste mesmo instante.

O trem enfim sai da estação.

Carla começa a ler um **livro** sobre **romance**, ao qual **suspira** pelo **personagem principal**, nesse meio tempo é **surpreendida** por um rapaz **alto** e **loiro**, muito educado e que chama a sua atenção.

- Moça, será que você poderia trocar de lugar comigo para que possa sentar ao lado de minha **mãe**? - Referindo-se a senhora sentada ao lado de Carla.

- Opa, claro. Posso trocar com o maior prazer, já estou ficando acostumada.

Ao trocar para a poltrona da frente, Carla estaria sentada **ao lado de** Roberto, que neste momento estava tentando ler o **jornal** do dia. **Nenhum** dos dois dá importância para o fato de estarem lado a lado.

O soldado Roberto é alto e grande, havia adquirido o assento de primeira classe achando que ganharia um lugar mais **espaçoso** que coubessem suas pernas. Nada disso aconteceu. O trem era **antigo** e a única coisa que muda de uma classe para a outra, era o fato de terem **comida e bebida** inclusas, além de um **travesseiro** bem desconfortável. Como não tinha muito espaço, começou a tentar se ajeitar na poltrona e logo despertou a atenção de Carla.

- Moço, estou te **atrapalhando**? – pergunta Carla.

- Me desculpe, é que não consigo achar um modo confortável de ficar nessas poltronas. - responde Roberto.

Nesse momento os dois se olham e bate uma **sensação** estranha em ambos. Carla fica **sem graça** por estar encarando o soldado e o mesmo acontece com ele. Ao tentar novamente se ajeitar, Roberto acaba deixando amostra um pedaço de fita que estaria em seu pulso, na cor verde que aparentava ter muitos anos. No mesmo instante, na mão de Carla, também havia uma fita idêntica; ambos se olharam quando perceberam o **inusitado** fato.

Carla fica estarrecida e muito **surpresa** com o acontecido e não para de olhar para fita no pulso de Roberto, o mesmo também se encontra surpreso e então fala para ela:

- Carlinha, é você mesmo? - pergunta Roberto.

- Inacreditável! Robertinho! – Carla por impulso abraça o soldado que fica afundado nos **braços** da pequena moça.

Acontece que por uma ajuda do **destino** ambos já se conheciam de um **acampamento** que participaram quando crianças em Budapeste. As fitas **simbolizavam** um casamento de mentirinha feito pelos dois na beira do **lago** onde brincavam juntos. Os dois achavam que quando adultos iriam se encontrar e casar para serem felizes para sempre.

Ao se darem conta do acontecido os dois não conseguiram parar de se olhar e Carla como uma boa tagarela não parava de falar, e Roberto não parava de se **encantar** com toda aquela conversa que estava acontecendo.

Nas três horas que seguiram de viagem, os dois se reencontraram, **trocaram** seus números de telefone, contaram sobre suas vidas e o sentimento que estava **adormecido** por anos re acendeu.

Resumo da história

Às vezes um simples engano pode mudar muita coisa. Carla cometeu um erro ao comprar seu bilhete de trem e acabou se surpreendendo muito com o resultado final. Como um encontro pode mudar toda uma vida? Roberto e Carla são velhos conhecidos que, apesar de terem tido suas vidas separadas, voltam a se encontrar anos depois. Quem diria que uma viagem de trem poderia render um encontro tão aleatório.

Summary of the story

Sometimes a simple mistake can change a lot. Carla made a mistake when she bought her train ticket and was very surprised by the final result. How can a meeting change a whole life? Roberto and Carla are old acquaintances who, despite having their lives separated, meet again years later. Who would have thought that a train trip could render such a random meeting?

Vocabulary

- **céu:** sky
- **cruzadas:** crossed
- **atrasado:** late
- **em tempo:** in time
- **trem:** train
- **soldado:** soldier
- **apartamento:** flat
- **bonita:** beautiful
- **cabelos castanhos claros:** light brown hair
- **banho:** bath
- **cronograma:** agenda
- **embarque:** boarding
- **primeira classe:** first class
- **conversar:** talk
- **sentado:** seated
- **bilhete:** ticket
- **funcionário:** employee
- **passageiros:** passengers
- **resolver:** to solve
- **defeito:** problem (defect)
- **envergonhada:** ashamed
- **possibilidade:** possibility
- **hoje:** today
- **acostumada:** be used to
- **argumentar:** to argue
- **adquirir:** to purchase
- **percebendo:** realizing
- **propõe:** propose
- **aborrecida:** annoyed
- **comprar:** to buy
- **gesticula:** gestures
- **acomoda:** acommodates
- **livro:** book
- **romance:** romance
- **suspira:** sighs
- **personagem principal:** main character
- **surpreendida:** surprised
- **alto:** tall
- **loiro:** blond
- **mãe:** mother
- **ao lado de:** next to
- **jornal:** newspaper
- **nenhum:** none
- **espaçoso:** spacious
- **antigo:** old
- **comida e bebida:** foods and drinks
- **travesseiro:** pillow
- **atrapalhando:** disturbing
- **sensação:** sensation
- **sem graça:** embarrassed
- **inusitado:** unusual
- **supresa:** surprise

- **braços:** arms
- **destino:** destination
- **acampamento:** camping
- **simbolizavam:** symbolized
- **lago:** lake
- **encantar:** to enchant
- **trocaram:** exchanged
- **adormecido:** asleep

Questions about the story

1. **Ambos pegaram taxis:**

   a. parecidos
   b. diferentes
   c. amarelos
   d. ocupados

2. **O trem em que estavam viajando para Budapeste era:**

   a. fraquinho
   b. antigo
   c. confortável
   d. pequeno

3. **Carla estava:**

   a. atrasada
   b. no horário
   c. cansada
   d. uniformizada

4. **O bilhete da viagem de Carla era:**

   a. para dois dias posteriores ao dia atual.
   b. para cinco dias anteriores ao dia atual.
   c. para três dias posteriores ao dia atual.
   d. para dois dias anteriores ao dia atual.

5. **Roberto e Carla tinham uma fita:**

   a. diferente
   b. amarela
   c. idêntica
   d. azul

Answers

1. B
2. B
3. A
4. C
5. C

CHAPTER EIGHT

INFINITIVE VERBS

Superar para amar - Overcome to love

Como de costume eu iria passar o **feriado** da **Páscoa** com meus avós na fazenda a pouco mais de duas horas da minha casa. Como já estava **namorando** há mais de um ano, chamei o Chico para ir comigo.

- Vamos, Chico, vai ser bem legal! Iremos **nadar** no rio, tentar **pescar** alguns peixes, fazer trilha até a cachoeira, será incrível. Vamos?

- Claro, Fernanda, eu topo!! Vamos de carro? – questionou Chico.

Naquele instante tive um **pressentimento ruim**, mas não dei muita importância e acabei **afirmando** que iriamos de carro até a fazenda.

No dia seguinte acordamos às sete da manhã e uma hora depois já estávamos na estrada. O percurso tem uma estrada boa, **dirigir** não é difícil. No instante em que entrei no carro, novamente pude sentir aquela sensação **estranha**, mas não dei importância. Quando faltavam apenas 20 km para chegar ao nosso destino um carro **desgovernado** nos atingiu em cheio. Depois disso, acordei somente no **hospital**.

À minha volta estavam meus avós, meus pais e nada do Chico! Quando comecei a reparar estava em um quarto de hospital, com vários **aparelhos** ligados em mim. Perguntei a todos o que tinha **acontecido.** Com muita **paciência** me explicaram sobre o **acidente** e foi então que reparei: havia perdido minha **perna esquerda.**

No momento quis muito gritar, **entrei em choque**, fiquei com tantos sentimentos de uma só vez que queria apenas **fugir** daquele lugar. Mas mesmo assim, quando olhei ao meu redor encontrei conforto. Meus pais estavam ali ao meu lado, esperando que eu acordasse; foi quando que olhei para meu avô que me disse:

- Deus está no meio de nós, ele irá te **proteger** de todo o mal, basta acreditar. Você perdeu uma perna, mas ainda tem a outra e vai **superar** todos os **obstáculos** que a vida trouxer. Você é uma **guerreira** minha neta, pode e deve se levantar e agradecer; está viva!

Com os olhos cheios de **lágrimas** senti um conforto enorme em meu coração. **Jamais** esqueci aquelas palavras, acreditar em mim mesma era necessário.

- Obrigada, vovô. Obrigada, **Deus**, pela minha vida. – disse em volta alta.

Após alguns dias consegui me recuperar e **receber alta** do hospital. A partir dali os meus dias nunca mais seriam os mesmos. Antes **sonhava** em ser **independente**, viajar, **casar**, **diplomar**, festejar, trabalhar; agora, estava aprendendo aos poucos a viver com minha nova realidade. Chico já estava em casa e me deu todo o **apoio** possível.

No momento eu tinha duas escolhas, ficar me **lamentando** pelo ocorrido e achar que a vida não era justa ou levantar minha cabeça e descobrir o mundo de possibilidades que estavam à minha frente. **Adivinhem** qual foi a escolha?

Ah, eu escolhi viver! **Agarrei-me** ao fato de ter uma família ótima, condições de superar os obstáculos e seguir com meu **tratamento** para ter a maior independência possível. Iniciei a **fisioterapia**, adaptação de **prótese**, etc.

Era difícil não ter mais um membro do meu corpo? Era, mas não era um fator determinante para que eu ficasse triste o tempo inteiro.

Conversando com o Chico tive a ideia de fazer uma viagem para praia, que era algo que queríamos fazer há muito tempo, antes mesmo do acidente.

- Chico, vamos à praia! Assim, posso perder esse medo que tenho de viajar novamente e posso aproveitar um pouco esse **mundo** tão bonito. – falei para meu **namorado**.

- Meu amor, você não acha cedo demais fazer uma viagem dessas? Não faz muito tempo desde o acidente, tem certeza disso? – perguntou Chico.

- Sim, **tenho certeza**. Tenho medo também, mas preciso **vencer** esse medo, a minha vida não pode parar por conta deste acidente, quero viver!! – respondi.

Um mês depois estávamos dentro de um avião rumo ao litoral para três dias de praia e paz.

Ao chegar no nosso destino, na pousada já notei um **gatinho** que não possuía uma das patas traseiras, mas que não se importava, caminhava, pedia carinho, e logo brinquei dizendo que havia achado um amiguinho parecido comigo. A dona da pousada disse que ele havia sido maltratado por uns garotos na rua e em decorrência dos ferimentos perdeu a **patinha**, mas que nunca se deixou abater.

Ali, ao invés de um pressentimento ruim, tive alguns muito bons e estava radiante. Na manhã seguinte, coloquei minha **roupa de praia** e acordei meu namorado cedinho para aproveitar o dia. No caminho até a praia, que era curto, as pessoas não paravam de olhar minha prótese; ouvi até uma senhora cochichar com outra – "nossa tão bonita e sem uma perna, que dó". Confesso que não gostei, mas decidi não dar importância.

- Olha, Chico! Que dia lindo, o sol está brilhante, vamos ter muitas horas de praia hoje. Está pronto? – conversei com Chico.

- Nossa, **realmente** nosso dia será de muita praia e **diversão**. Esse dia foi feito para você, meu amor!! – Chico respondeu para mim.

Ao chegar à areia da praia, mais uma grande novidade que me deixa muito surpresa: um dos **surfistas** presentes não possuía um de seus braços. Nossa, assim que olhei achei curioso e fui ao encontro do surfista, que se chamava Jack e era natural daquela cidade.

Conversei muito com ele, fiquei **admirada** em ver como ele conseguia surfar, e me dei conta de que tudo é uma questão de adaptação, assim como ele fez para superar sua **dor** e dificuldades para continuar a fazer o que gosta, surfar.

Passamos o dia na praia, Jack até tentou me ensinar a surfar, mas acho que ainda terei que **praticar** bastante para conseguir. Mesmo assim o dia foi muito bom e divertido, conheci pessoas **maravilhosas** e me dei conta de que encontrei em meu caminho **exemplos** admiráveis. Nunca deixei de sonhar ou acreditar em mim mesma e um fator determinante para isso foi estar sempre pensando **positivamente**.

Após aquela viagem decidi tornar a minha voz em prol dos **deficientes** mais ativa. Comecei a dar **palestras** e contar a minha história ao redor do mundo, levar para os mais diferentes lugares **pensamentos** e **motivações** que iriam fazer as pessoas mais felizes e corajosas. Na maioria das vezes, tudo que uma pessoa precisa é de **conforto emocional** para seguir em frente.

Resumo da história

Muitas vezes a vida muda tão de repente que precisamos entender que não temos o controle de tudo, e a escolha de continuar lutando e não desistir de viver independente da situação não é fácil. Mas com o apoio das pessoas certas é possível. Fernanda teve que aprender a lidar com uma mudança brusca em seu corpo após um acidente, mas com a ajuda da sua família e de seu namorado, teve forças para seguir em frente.

Summary of the story

Many times, life changes so suddenly that we need to understand we do not have control of everything and the choice to continue fighting and not giving up living, inspite of the situation, is not easy; but with the support of the right people it is possible. Fernanda had to learn how to deal with a sudden change in her body after an accident, but with the help of her family and her boyfriend she had the strength to move on.

Vocabulary

- **como de costume:** as usual
- **feriado:** holiday
- **Páscoa:** Easter
- **namorando:** dating
- **nadar:** to swim
- **pescar:** to fish (verb)
- **pressentimento ruim:** bad feeling
- **afirmando:** stating
- **dirigir:** to drive
- **estranha:** strange
- **desgovernado:** unruly
- **hospital:** hospital
- **aparelhos:** equipment
- **acontecido:** happened
- **paciência:** patience
- **acidente:** accident
- **perna esquerda:** left leg
- **entrei em choque:** I went into shock
- **fugir:** to run away
- **proteger:** to protect
- **superar:** to overcome
- **obstáculos:** obstacles
- **guerreira:** warrior
- **lágrimas:** tears
- **jamais:** never
- **Deus:** God
- **receber alta:** discharge
- **sonhava:** dreamed
- **independente:** independent
- **casar:** to get married
- **diplomar:** to graduate
- **apoio:** support
- **lamentando:** regretting
- **advinhem:** guess
- **agarrei:** I held
- **tratamento:** treatment
- **fisioterapia:** physiotherapy
- **prótese:** prosthesis
- **mundo:** world
- **namorado:** boyfriend
- **tenho certeza:** I am sure
- **vencer:** to win
- **gatinho:** kitty
- **patinha:** little pawn
- **roupa de praia:** swimsuit
- **realmente:** really
- **diversão:** fun
- **surfistas:** surfers
- **admirada:** surprised
- **dor:** pain
- **praticar:** to practice

81

- **maravilhosas:** wonderful
- **exemplos:** examples
- **positivamente:** positively
- **deficientes:** disabled
- **palestras:** lectures

- **pensamentos:** thoughts
- **motivações:** motivation
- **conforto emocional:** emotional comfort

Questions about the story

1. **Fernanda iria para a fazenda para:**

   a. passar o natal

   b. passar o fim de semana

   c. passar o feriado de Páscoa

   d. passar as férias

2. **Antes de viajar para a fazenda Fernanda:**

   a. ficou nervosa

   b. teve um mau pressentimento

   c. não queria ir

   d. não chamou Chico

3. **Após acordar Fernanda começou a:**

   a. gritar de dor

   b. reparar que estava em um hospital

   c. fugir para escapar dali

   d. ficar em choque

4. **O avô de Fernanda disse que ela deve:**

   a. proteger e acreditar em si mesma

   b. superar os obstáculos encontrados

   c. se levantar e agradecer porque está viva.

   d. se recuperar e receber alta do hospital.

5. **Os sonhos de Fernanda eram:**

   a. ser dependente, casar e trabalhar.

   b. viajar e ficar se lamentando pelo ocorrido.

   c. não trabalhar mais, ser dependente e viajar.

   d. viajar, casar e festejar.

Answers

1. C
2. B
3. B
4. C
5. D

CHAPTER NINE

FORMAL AND INFORMAL LANGUAGE

De Paris ao Vidigal - From Paris to Vidigal

Em uma tarde **ensolarada** com um clima excepcional, **decidi** que iria realizar um **coquetel** para meus amigos **íntimos**, comemorando o **sucesso** do meu novo **livro** sobre minha viagem até o **continente** da Oceania.

Como bom **escritor**, faço novas **amizades** e ouço todo tipo de história por onde ando; como quando **conheci** o doutor Luiz, **responsável** por uma das **pesquisas** mais conceituadas da **atualidade** sobre a cura do vitiligo. Com certeza irei convidá-lo. Outro **conhecido**, que tenho grande **consideração**, é o Seu Chico, dono da **banca de jornais** próximo a minha residência. Tenho muito carinho por este companheiro. Cabra-macho!

Convido vários amigos e seus acompanhantes, a noite será **esplêndida**. Convoco meus melhores **empregados** e decido por um menu **diversificado**, para agradar a todos. Nas bebidas, teremos de caipirinha a prosecco francês; no bufê, optei por comidas **leves** e saborosas. O evento estava **marcado** para às oito horas no jardim de minha casa, que acabara de reformar.

- Senhor, devo anunciar a chegada do Sr. Armando Lúcio. – disse o **mordomo**.

- Pontualidade, Hein? Obrigado por avisar. – Neste **momento,** dirijo-me até a porta para recebê-lo.

- Como tem passado Sr. Armando? E vossa **esposa** já se recuperou da **cirurgia**?

- Meu caro amigo, André! Que bom estar contigo nessa **celebração.** Meus parabéns pelo sucesso do novo livro. Agradeço por perguntar, minha belíssima esposa encontra-se ainda em **recuperação**, mas enviou a você as mais sinceras felicitações. – disse o Sr. Armando, famoso **joalheiro** da cidade.

- Muito agradecido, meu amigo! Por favor, **fique à vontade**, aproveite para passear pelo **jardim**, realizei modificações formidáveis.

Enquanto o Senhor Armando passeia pelo jardim, aproveito para finalizar os últimos **ajustes** na **trilha sonora** que tocará no coquetel. Nessa hora, me deparo com a diversidade das pessoas que convidei. Hoje iriam **comparecer** desde pessoas que possuem gosto pela música clássica até amigos que apreciam um bom samba! Caramba, isso será um desafio: agradar a todos.

Começam a chegar mais convidados. Nessa hora **avisto** uma velha amiga de faculdade, a Cidinha, famosa pela gargalhada alta e **vocabulário** esdrúxulo. Sempre muito bem vestida e inteligente, tornou-se uma das mais importantes **editoras** do país, comandava o jornal de maior circulação da capital. Neste momento vou até seu encontro.

- Olá, Cidinha! Que **vestido** belo, está lindíssima! Como vai? – Faço festa pela sua chegada.

- Fala, Dedeco! Quanta **formalidade**, venha aqui me dá um abraço!

- Opa, estou sendo amassado, Cidinha!!

- Dedeco, estou muito feliz pelo seu sucesso. Aqui, ó, trouxe o livro para ganhar um **autógrafo**. Que festa de arromba, obrigada pelo convide! (muitas gargalhadas podem ser ouvidas nesse momento).

- Claro que autografo, minha grande amiga. Fique à vontade, tem **cerveja** e caipirinha no bar, pode escolher! Ah, meu jardim está de cara nova, vá lá conferir!!

Pego o livro de Cidinha e levo para o escritório onde irei **assinar** e devolver para minha amiga que já está se enturmando com a galera do bar.

O meu livro estava entre os mais vendidos em algumas das **livrarias** que frequento. Minha felicidade estava estampada em minha cara. Nessa viagem para a Oceania conheci pessoas e culturas totalmente diferentes. Por sorte e um amigo em comum, conheci o **Embaixador** do Brasil na Austrália, participei de jantares na embaixada... enfim, me tornei amigo de uma grande pessoa e de sua família, que por coincidência estavam passando **férias** no Brasil. Logo, foram convidados para meu coquetel. Os Costa e Silva chegaram pontualmente, assim como Sr. Armando. Pude ir até à porta e recebe-los com muita compaixão.

- **Boa noite** meus queridos, conseguiram achar o **endereço** conforme repassei? – Abraço a todos com muito respeito, pois são uma família muito fina e reservada.

- Claro, André. Sua casa é formidável, uma das mais bonitas e relevantes da quadra, foi fácil encontrá-la. – disse o Embaixador Eduardo.

- Vossa Excelência, fique à vontade, sinta-se em casa.

- Sim, e deixe de formalidade "Dedeco", aqui somos todos amigos! Onde está a cerveja? – retrucou o embaixador.

- Beleza, Dudu! A cerveja você pode pegar no bar, **novamente**, fique à vontade.

Como bom **anfitrião** tenho que conseguir dividir meu tempo com todos os convidados e dedicar um pouco do meu tempo para cada um deles. Apesar da noite ser de **comemoração**, gosto de cada um que está presente.

Neste momento olho ao redor e vejo que algumas pessoas já começaram a conhecer umas às outras. Por exemplo, Cidinha já estava conversando com o Embaixador e sua esposa, enquanto o Sr. Armando batia o maior papo com o Seu Chico da banca.

Para minha grande surpresa, minha mãe conseguiu vir de Paris para o coquetel; fiz o convite, mas sinceramente achei que não iria aparecer. Dona Emília é uma mulher admirável, com muitos encantos, geralmente, se torna o **centro das atenções** onde quer que vá. Chegou com toda a sua fineza e atraiu o olhar de todos com seu belo sorriso (nessa parte a genética ajudou, o meu é idêntico).

- André Valois, minha joia rara! Achou que eu iria perder sua comemoração?

Neste momento, Dona Emília deixa de lado as formalidades e me abraça como se não me visse há muito tempo (o que era verdade) e me enche de **beijos**. Fico muito feliz!

- Estou surpreso sim, mãe! Porém, muito feliz! Deixou seu lar em Paris para me prestigiar!! – respondo a Dona Emília.

- Deixa de ser bobo, você é muito mais importante do que uma taça de champanhe no topo da Torre Eiffel. Aliás, tem champanhe no seu coquetel? Vou à procura.

- Está bem, mamãe. No bar você vai **encontrar** o que procura!!

Deixo Dona Emília no bar e caminho até o jardim que está belíssimo, a **reforma** ficou magnífica. Vou até a mesa onde preparei um **curta-metragem** para mostrar aos convidados as partes que mais admiro no meu livro, afinal além de escritor sou um ótimo fotógrafo. Com um balançar e toque de taças chamo a atenção de todos e faço um breve discurso.

- Meus caros e seletos amigos, devo admitir que estou muito emocionado e feliz com a presença de todos e é **inenarrável** a felicidade que sinto pelo **reconhecimento** do meu trabalho, afinal foram **meses** de preparação para tentar repassar todos os momentos magníficos que pude presenciar e viver no continente que agora estará sempre em meu **coração**, a Oceania. Neste breve curta-metragem irei mostrar cenas inéditas de alguns passeios e os bastidores de alguns momentos retratados no livro. Espero que apreciem, assim como eu os aprecio. Seu Chico, preste atenção ao final, em uma **vila** consegui filmar os sons musicais que eram feitos pelos locais, algo que vai lembrar-lhe daquele sambinha da semana passada lá no Vidigal! Eles riem.

Como já havia visto o curta, decido **dedicar** meus olhares aos convidados. Fico emocionado como todos prestam atenção e alguns até se emocionam igual a mim. Caramba, é muito bom viver e **trabalhar** com o que a gente gosta!

O restante do coquetel foi um sucesso, todos estavam muito felizes e entrosados, foi ótimo. Espero que meu livro sobre o litoral do Brasil tenha o mesmo sucesso!

Resumo da história

André é um escritor de renome que quer fazer um coquetel de lançamento de seu livro de sucesso sobre a viagem ao continente oceânico. Mesmo sendo um homem letrado, o escritor se relaciona com todo o tipo de gente. São pessoas com as quais passou alguns momentos de sua vida, e o desafio agora será agradar aos convidados e fazer do coquetel um evento de sucesso.

Summary of the story

Andre is a renowned writer who wants to make a cocktail of his successful book launch on his voyage to the oceanic continent. Even as a literate man, the writer relates to all kinds of people, people with whom he spent a few moments of his life and the challenge now will be to please the guests and make the cocktail event a success.

Vocabulary

- **ensolarada:** sunny
- **decidi:** decided
- **coquetel:** cocktail
- **amigos íntimos:** close friends
- **sucesso:** success
- **continente:** continent
- **escritor:** writer
- **amizades:** friendships
- **conheci:** got to know
- **responsável:** responsible
- **pesquisas:** researches
- **atualidade:** present
- **conhecido:** acquainted
- **consideração:** consideration
- **banca de jornais:** newsstand
- **esplêndida:** splendid
- **empregados:** employees
- **diversificado:** diverse
- **leves:** light
- **marcado:** scheduled
- **mordomo:** butler
- **momento:** moment
- **esposa:** wife
- **cirurgia:** surgery
- **celebração:** celebration
- **recuperação:** recovery
- **joalheiro:** jeweler
- **fique à vontade:** make yourself at home
- **jardim:** garden
- **ajustes:** settings
- **trilha sonora:** soundtrack
- **comparecer:** attend
- **avisto:** catch sight of
- **vocabulário:** vocabulary
- **editoras:** editors
- **vestido:** dress
- **formalidade:** formality
- **autógrafo:** autograph
- **cerveja:** beer
- **assinar:** sign
- **livrarias:** bookstores
- **Embaixador:** Ambassador
- **férias:** vacations
- **boa noite:** good evening
- **endereço:** address
- **novamente:** once again
- **anfitrião:** host
- **comemoração:** celebration
- **centro das atenções:** center of attentions
- **beijos:** kisses

- **encontrar:** to find
- **reforma:** renovation
- **curta-metragem:** short film
- **inenarrável:** unspeakable
- **reconhecimento:** recognition
- **meses:** months

- **coração:** heart
- **vila:** village
- **dedicar:** to dedicate
- **trabalhar:** to work

Questions about the story

1. **"Seu Chico" é o uso informal de:**

   a. Senhor Francisco

   b. Senhora Francisca

   c. Senhorita Chica

   d. Idoso Francisco

2. **No texto, o termo Cabra-macho significa:**

   a. criador de cabras

   b. corajoso, decidido, valente

   c. sujeito homem

   d. um companheiro carinhoso

3. **O jardim de André passou por uma reforma e estava:**

   a. explêndido e idêntico

   b. agradecido e entusiasmado

   c. formidável e de cara nova

   d. entrosado e inenarrável

4. **"Dedeco" é um apelido, o uso informal de:**

   a. Derick

   b. Delfran

   c. Delson

   d. André

5. **Segundo o texto, chegaram pontualmente ao coquetel:**

   a. Dona Emília e Cidinha

   b. Os Costa e Silva e Sr. Armando

   c. Seu Chico e Dona Emília

   d. Sr. Armando e Dona Emília

Answers

1. A
2. B
3. C
4. D
5. B

CHAPTER TEN

ADVERBS

Uma noite inesquecível – An unforgettable night

Já eram quase cinco da **tarde** quando recebo uma **mensagem** no **celular**. Era minha melhor amiga com um convite **irrecusável**, o **espetáculo** de um grupo de teatro muito **famoso** da **cidade**, em cartaz com uma peça sobre como sobreviver à vida **adulta,** que prometia ser hilária.

Logo **respondo** aceitando o **convite**. Marcamos de nos **encontrarmos** às sete e meia em frente ao **teatro**. Meu **expediente** costuma terminar às seis horas, portanto, consigo chegar ao teatro com tempo de sobra. De repente recebo uma **ligação** bastante inesperada, meu **ex-namorado** me liga de Nova Iorque. "O que esse **rapaz** quer comigo? Não me **esquece** mesmo...". Resolvo atender a ligação, pois ainda estava no **escritório**.

- Alô, **quem fala?** (finjo não saber quem é).

- Oi, Maria, tudo bem? Aqui é o Márcio, estou com saudades suas, como você está?

- Oi, Márcio, nossa quanto tempo! Estou esplêndida e você? "**Congelando**" nos Estados Unidos?

- Está tudo lindo, muito **agradável** o tempo por aqui! Bom, vou falar a verdade, estou ligando para pedir um **favor**. Acredita que o rapaz que ficou de colocar **ração** para o meu **gato** não poderá ir?! Por favor, você poderia ir até lá e fazer isso para mim? A **chave** está naquele velho esconderijo. Muito obrigado, Mah, vou ter que desligar...

- Mas, Márcio, estou de saída. Márcio? Alô?...

A ligação já havia se encerrado.

Neste momento eu me deparo com uma **situação** horrível, não posso deixar o gato morrer de **fome**, mas também, por que faria isso para o Márcio, ele **terminou** comigo por um motivo bobo; até hoje não entendi direito.

Como eu tenho o **coração** mole, no fim penso mais no gato do que no louco do meu ex-namorado. Resolvo ir até a casa dele e rapidamente colocar comida para o gato para enfim ir ao teatro correndo.

- Caramba, como eu sou **azarada**, se não me apressar chegarei atrasada ao teatro e a Julinha vai me matar - penso.

Apresso o passo e pego um táxi até a casa do Márcio. Quando entro no táxi sou recebida com um boa noite em tom bem **charmoso** e calmo.

- Boa noite, Senhora. Ou devo corrigir, Senhorita? – disse o taxista charmoso.

- Boa noite. E, sim, é senhorita! A vida não está favorável para mudar o pronome de tratamento.

- Não fale assim, você apenas não achou o cara certo!

- Obrigada. Podemos nos apressar? Tenho dois **compromissos** hoje e já estou atrasada para o segundo!!

- Claro, ao seu dispor, porém, tenho que **respeitar** as leis de **trânsito.** Além de a senhorita chegar ao destino tem que chegar bem, não é?

- Sim, muito obrigada por lembrar, **dirija** com prudência!

Nesse momento começo a mandar **mensagem** para Julinha explicando o que estava acontecendo, mas me pego descrevendo o motorista, um rapaz que achei charmoso demais. Começo então a me arrumar para o teatro ali no carro mesmo, passar **batom**, um pouco de **maquiagem**... O **cabelo** já estava um horror, não tinha muito o que mudar.

Pegamos um pequeno engarrafamento muito próximo à casa de Márcio, então comecei a ficar agitada com a demora. O taxista como sempre muito **educado** tenta me acalmar.

- Calma senhorita, vamos chegar daqui a pouco, afinal o prédio é logo ali e toda essa produção fica ainda melhor com um **sorriso** no rosto. – disse o motorista.

Nossa, nessa hora fico tão vermelha, mas **confesso** que gostei do elogio.

- Obrigada, vou sorrir mais! - respondo.

Ao chegarmos **à frente** do prédio pago a corrida rapidamente e saio do carro correndo em direção à portaria. O porteiro me reconheceu, mas ficou desconfiado, pois não havia recebido **nenhuma** ordem para deixar que eu subisse até o **apartamento**. Exigiu que o Márcio autorizasse minha entrada.

Por sorte consegui mandar uma mensagem, e Márcio enviou um **recado por voz** para o porteiro, que finalmente deixou que eu entrasse. Achei a chave, fiz carinho no gato, coloquei sua comida e estava tudo certo para continuar minha **jornada** até o teatro.

Novamente na frente do prédio, peço outro táxi para chegar ao teatro no horário marcado, mas em nenhum momento anterior àquele olhei a hora. Quando o fiz levei um susto, pois estava muito atrasada!

O táxi chega e fico mais tranquila quando já estou a caminho do teatro. A corrida é ótima, o senhor que me levou era super educado e o trânsito estava cooperando.

Ao chegar em frente ao teatro, o motorista me diz o valor da corrida e começo a procurar a minha **carteira** para efetuar o **pagamento**, quando me deparo com um tremendo susto: ela não estava lá!

Começo a entrar em **desespero** e o motorista recebe outra corrida para fazer. Isso eu consegui resolver, pois chamei Julinha aos gritos (que vergonha) e ela pagou a corrida para mim.

Como já havíamos **perdido** a sessão do teatro resolvi sentar e tomar um copo de água para tentar me acalmar. Foi quando me lembrei da corrida de táxi até a casa de Márcio e de que havia pagado o motorista charmoso. Agora, como eu poderia resolver essa questão? Minha amiga teve uma ideia:

- Maria, ligue agora para a companhia de táxi. Nós temos a **descrição** do motorista, lembra que você fez isso nas mensagens?

- É verdade. Vou tentar.

Ligo então para a **companhia de táxi** e com os dados das mensagens consegui dizer o horário em que estava no carro e quando saí, pois, estava **fofocando** tudo para Julinha. A atendente da companhia escuta toda a minha **trajetória** e fica impressionada com os detalhes que repasso sobre o motorista. Por sorte ela também sabia de quem estávamos falando - aparentemente ele era gentil e educado com todos, e se chamava Valter.

Fico **extremamente** feliz quando a atendente retorna minha ligação e confirma que a carteira estava no carro do Senhor Valter. Ela me passa o telefone dele e eu ligo quase que no mesmo instante. Combinamos um ponto de encontro para a entrega.

Eu e Júlia nós **direcionamos** até o ponto de encontro, uma **lanchonete** próxima ao teatro. Valter chega um bom tempo depois e revela que não tinha visto a carteira até a atendente entrar em contato com ele; e que já estava no caminho de casa, do outro lado da cidade.

Caramba! Atrapalhei o percurso do motorista, por **falha** minha e pelo meu nervosismo. No final percebi que não podemos querer fazer mil **tarefas** ao mesmo tempo e que fazer as coisas com mais calma é sempre melhor. **Agradeci** muito ao motorista e lhe ofereci uma recompensa. No entanto, ele não aceitou.

Por fim, fui com a Júlia a um bar próximo de onde estávamos e **comecei** a contar novamente toda a história. Na mesa atrás da nossa estavam os produtores da **peça** que riram muito do ocorrido e nos deram dois ingressos para a sessão de amanhã.

O gato não passou fome, a correria não adiantou de nada, mas ganhei os **ingressos** para a peça que tanto queria assistir. No fim, tudo se acertou, e a pressa... de nada adiantou.

Resumo da história

Todo mundo sabe que não é recomendável fazer muitas tarefas ao mesmo tempo. Dizem que a pressa é inimiga da perfeição, e talvez seja mesmo. Em alguns momentos é preciso relaxar e ter mais calma. É o caso de Maria, que muda todos os seus planos para ajudar Márcio, mas acaba se atrasando e perdendo um compromisso com sua amiga Julia. Maria aprende uma valiosa lição.

Summary of the story

Everyone knows that doing many tasks at the same time is not recommended. They say that haste is the enemy of perfection and maybe it is. At times you need to relax and take it easy. This is the case of Maria, who changes all her plans to help Marcio, but ends up being late and losing a meeting she had with her friend Julia. Mary learns a valuable lesson.

Vocabulary

- **tarde:** afternoon
- **mensagem:** message
- **celular:** cell phone
- **irrecusável:** irrecusable
- **espetáculo:** show
- **famoso:** famous
- **cidade:** city
- **adulta:** adult
- **respondo:** reply
- **convite:** invitation
- **encontrarmos:** find
- **teatro:** theater
- **expediente:** working hours
- **ligação:** call
- **ex-namorado:** ex-boyfriend
- **rapaz:** boy
- **esquece:** forget
- **escritório:** office
- **quem fala?:** who's there?
- **congelando:** freezing
- **agradável:** pleasant
- **favor:** favor
- **ração:** animal food
- **gato:** cat
- **chave:** key
- **situação:** situation
- **fome:** hunger
- **terminou:** broke up
- **coração:** heart
- **azarada:** unlucky
- **charmoso:** charming
- **compromissos:** appointments
- **respeitar:** to respect
- **trânsito:** traffic
- **dirija:** drive
- **mensagem:** message
- **batom:** lipstick
- **maquiagem:** make-up
- **cabelo:** hair
- **educado:** polite
- **sorriso:** smile
- **confesso:** confess
- **na frente:** in front of
- **nenhuma:** any
- **apartamento:** apartment
- **recado por voz:** voice note
- **jornada:** journey
- **carteira:** wallet
- **pagamento:** payment
- **desespero:** desperation
- **perdido:** lost
- **descrição:** description

- **companhia de táxi:** taxi company
- **fofocando:** gossiping
- **trajetória:** trajectory
- **extremamente:** extremely
- **direcionamos:** headed
- **lanchonete:** snack bar
- **falha:** failure
- **tarefas:** tasks
- **agradeci:** thanked
- **comecei:** started
- **peça:** play
- **ingressos:** tickets

Questions about the story

1. **Qual foi o convite irrecusável que Maria aceitou?**
    a. um espetáculo de sua melhor amiga
    b. uma peça do grupo de teatro muito famoso
    c. um espetáculo em Nova Yorque
    d. uma peça sobre como ser hilário

2. **Qual foi a situação muito inesperada que Maria passou?**
    a. Mário, seu ex namorado ligando de Nova Yorque
    b. Márcio ligando de Nova Jersey e pedindo um favor
    c. Márcio ligando e pedindo um favor
    d. Mário congelando nos Estados Unidos

3. **Por que Maria está azarada?**
    a. porque Julinha vai matá-la
    b. porque vai se apressar ao teatro
    c. porque precisa chegar no horário ao teatro
    d. porque perdeu os bilhetes para ir ao teatro

4. **Maria se atrasou mais ainda porque o porteiro do prédio:**
    a. exigiu sua identidade e trancou a porta
    b. exigiu que Márcio autorizasse a entrada
    c. estava no horário de almoço
    d. subiu no apartamento

5. **O que Julia esqueceu no táxi?**
    a. o celular
    b. a bolsa
    c. o ingresso
    d. a carteira

Answers

1. B
2. C
3. C
4. B
5. D

CHAPTER ELEVEN

TIME, DATE AND CLIMATE

Férias chegando - Vacations are coming

O **final do ano** está chegando e junto com ele as **férias escolares** que tanto espero. Marquei com Júnior (meu irmão) de começar nossa **viagem** até a casa de nossos pais no final da tarde, no máximo até as sete horas da noite, com isso podemos viajar tranquilos durante a **madrugada** e chegar logo pela manhã.

- Marina, está tudo pronto para começarmos a viagem? Está levando **casaco**? Olhei a estimativa de temperatura e estará **frio** por lá – perguntou Júnior.

- Boa, Júnior. Não estava, mas combinei com nossa mãe de ir por volta das duas horas da tarde no **shopping** comprar roupas para o fim do ano, aproveito e compro novos casacos, pois aqui em Brasília está uma mistura de clima **chuvoso** com calor.

- Está bem, mas lembre-se de que você não irá pegar os meus casacos **emprestados**, da última vez você devolveu todos encardidos. – **reclama** Júnior.

Para deixar claro, eu e Júnior passamos em concursos públicos e os escritórios estão situados em Brasília, mas nossa terra natal é no **interior** de Minas Gerais. Claro, passei primeiro do que ele e me mudei para cá, com isso Júnior não aguentou de saudades e fez o mesmo.

O clima em Brasília é bem **seco**, existem épocas do ano em que o **nariz** chega a **sangrar** devido as alterações climáticas e em outras o **guarda-chuva** na **bolsa** é indispensável, pois pode chover a qualquer momento e minutos depois o sol aparece e fica um tremendo calor. Geralmente no final da tarde lá pelas cinco horas começam os chuviscos que podem durar por tempo indeterminado.

Com as **malas** prontas, tomo meu último café às quatro e quinze e vou de táxi até o apartamento de meu irmão que não fica muito **longe** do meu. Quando cheguei lá, Júnior ainda não terminara de fazer as suas malas e pede mais quinze minutos para finalizar. Após esse período entramos no carro dele e iniciamos nossa viagem; como é final de ano as estradas estão cheias, por isso também decidimos sair nesse horário.

Como disse anteriormente, começa a **chover** exatamente às cinco e vinte, as pistas ficam **molhadas**, e o limpador do carro de Júnior está horrível, não limpa nada direito, paramos então para fazer a troca das palhetas em uma loja de acessórios, nisso já atrasamos mais meia hora do percurso.

Assim que voltamos à pista, a chuva para e o sol aparece (com o horário de verão demora mais um pouco para escurecer na cidade). Retomamos a estrada e tudo ocorre tranquilamente, começa a anoitecer e paramos em um posto para jantar.

- Nossa, Marina, já estou cansado de dirigir, você poderia continuar o caminho restante para mim? Só faltam duas horas para chegarmos. – **pergunta** Júnior.

- Já está cansado? Esses jovens de hoje em dia. Termino o trajeto sim, pode ir dormindo, já está de noite mesmo.

Viro a **motorista** da vez, coloco uma **música** bem animada para me manter acordada durante a madrugada, a pista está bem engarrafada e houve um acidente logo a frente, por tanto as duas horas que faltavam se transformam em, no mínimo, quatro horas.

Finalmente chegamos até onde **moram** nossos pais, tudo continua como era antes. Em cidades pequenas você acaba conhecendo e reconhecendo todo mundo; como chegamos por volta das seis da manhã, resolvo passar na padaria para comprar pão para o café da manhã e o dono do lugar já nos conhece.

- Estão chegando os filhos do Dr. Felipe, como estão? Marina e Júnior! Chegaram quando, agora? - pergunta o Seu José da padaria.

- Tudo bem, sim, chegamos agora na cidade e decidimos comprar um **pãozinho** para o café da manhã. Tem algum saindo do **forno**? – respondo para ele.

- Ah, e aquele pão de queijo? Ainda tem por aí Seu Zé? – Pergunta Junior para ele.

- Sim e sim. Posso atender todos esses pedidos. Como está Brasília, muito frio naquela cidade?

- Está chovendo um pouco, mas está é calor por lá! Júnior responde para ele.

- Pois é, Júnior. Aqui em Montes Claros está muito frio, estou dormindo com duas **cobertas**, acredita? Respondi Seu Zé.

Nesse momento o padeiro já estava com os nossos pedidos nas sacolinhas e então nos despedimos, nos dirigimos para o caixa e pagamos a conta.

Ao chegar na casa de nossos pais somos recebidos por todos os três **cachorros** que começam a latir de emoção como em todas as vezes que nos encontram. Todos já estão velhinhos, devem ter mais de dez anos de idade.

Logo meu pai vem nos receber, ainda com cara de sono, acho que chegamos muito cedo.

- Meus filhos, que surpresa, chegaram!! Entrem, vou chamar a mãe de vocês, ela está começando a fazer o café.

Ufa, pelo menos chegamos na hora certa, a mais de trinta anos meus pais acordam as seis da manhã e tomam café juntos e leem as notícias do **jornal** ou assistem pela televisão.

Ao entrar na casa existe todo aquele sentimento de nostalgia, aquela era a casa onde passamos a maior parte de nossas vidas e é sempre bom retornar, não importa se está frio, quente, chovendo demais, calor demais, será sempre nossa cidade do coração.

Quando mamãe nos encontra começa a sessão de abraços e apertos e é claro os famosos comentários: "Está muito magra, tem de comer mais." "Júnior está muito fofinho, só come besteira, né?".

Logo nos sentamos todos à mesa e começamos a colocar os **assuntos** em dia. Meu pai colocou na cabeça que irá no próximo ano realizar uma **temporada** de pesca com seus amigos, mais precisamente na época de primavera que é quando ele diz que tem mais peixes no rio. Minha mãe resolveu entrar na faculdade de **enfermagem** para ajudar mais na comunidade da cidade, já estava até programando seus próximos quatros anos para não interferir nas aulas. Os dois estão muito empolgados com os novos planos, e muito felizes!

Os dias que passamos por lá foram importantes por trazerem uma paz e descanso imenso pelo menos para mim, mas acredito que Júnior se sinta da mesma forma. O tempo naquela cidade parece passar mais **devagar**, ficamos por ali de vinte e dois de dezembro até três de janeiro, aproveitamos bastante.

Quando retornamos para Brasília já estamos felizes e revigorados para iniciar mais um novo ano, neste caso o de 2019. Devo confessar que o ano de 2018 foi muito acelerado e que no próximo decidi fazer as coisas com mais atenção, porém com mais calma do que antes.

Resumo da história

Marina e Junior são dois irmãos indo visitar os pais e viver a nostalgia da infância que tiveram ali. Alguns imprevistos climáticos e de horário fazem mudanças no ritmo da viagem de carro até lá, mas no final eles reencontram pessoas queridas, presenciam o fim da primavera e conseguem matar a saudade dos pais.

Summary of the story

Marina and Junior are two brothers going to visit their parents and live the nostalgia of the childhood they had there. Some unpredictable climate and time changes affect the rhythm of the car trip, but in the end, they meet up with loved ones, they witness the end of spring and they manage to kill the homesickness of their parents.

Vocabulary

- **final do ano:** end of the year
- **férias escolares:** school vacations
- **viagem:** trip
- **madrugada:** late night
- **casaco:** coat
- **frio:** cold
- **shopping:** mall
- **chuvoso:** rainy
- **emprestados:** borrowed
- **reclama:** complains
- **interior:** countryside
- **seco:** dry
- **nariz:** nose
- **sangrar:** to bleed
- **guarda-chuva:** umbrella
- **bolsa:** purse
- **malas:** luggages
- **longe:** far
- **chover:** to rain
- **molhadas:** wet
- **pergunta:** asks
- **motorista:** driver
- **música:** music
- **moram:** live
- **pãozinho:** small bread
- **forno:** oven
- **cobertas:** blanket
- **cachorros:** dogs
- **jornal:** newspaper
- **assuntos:** subjects
- **temporada:** season
- **enfermagem:** nursing
- **devagar:** slow

Questions about the story

1. **Qual, segundo o texto, era o melhor horário para os dois viajarem tranquilos?**
   a. durante a madrugada e chegar pela manhã
   b. durante a noite e chegar pela manhã
   c. durante a tarde e chegar pela noite
   d. durante a noite e chegar pela madrugada

2. **Como está o tempo em Brasília antes da viagem?**
   a. frio e chuvoso
   b. seco e frio
   c. seco e quente
   d. chuvoso e calor

3. **Quantos minutos Junior pede para terminar de arrumar as malas?**
   a. doze
   b. quinze
   c. dez
   d. cinco

4. **Qual foi o horário da chegada em Montes Claros?**
   a. às três da manhã
   b. às seis da manhã
   c. às oito da manhã
   d. às sete da manhã

5. **Qual foi o período em que Marina e Junior visitaram os pais em Montes Claros?**
   a. de vinte e cinco de dezembro a nove de janeiro
   b. de vinte e dois de dezembro até oito de janeiro
   c. de vinte e dois de dezembro até três de janeiro
   d. de vinte e três de janeiro até dois de fevereiro

Answers

1. A
2. D
3. B
4. B
5. C

CHAPTER TWELVE

FOOD AND DRINKS

Bar Aurora: A diversão começa aqui -
Bar Aurora - The fun starts here

Final da faculdade de **administração**, o **estágio** acabando, as contas chegando e eu ainda não tinha uma ideia **revolucionária** na cabeça. Estava começando a me **preocupar**, quando fui com alguns amigos em um bar na Rua Conceição, próximo da faculdade.

Este local era famoso por seus drinks e **coquetéis** tradicionais, mas feitos com maestria pelo rapaz que comandava o bar. Estava sempre **lotado**, a **cerveja** era barata, os coquetéis sem **álcool** também eram bem famosos e, é claro, tinham os quitutes de Dona Maria. Ela fazia desde pastéis de **diversos** sabores a picanha com mandioca na chapa, era tudo uma delícia.

Sempre que eu ia lá com os meus amigos nosso **pedido** era o mesmo, cerveja para os que não estavam dirigindo e suco de acerola para quem era o motorista da vez. Para beliscar sempre tinha as porções de **salame** e para quem estava com muita fome tinha o hambúrguer de costela; o pedido raramente mudava.

Quando estávamos todos **reunidos** e conversando, percebi que podia comandar um lugar parecido com aquele, mas com um diferencial: seria um bar que fecharia um pouco mais tarde e estaria próximo das principais baladas da cidade, como se fosse uma espécie de **ponto de encontro** para os mais diversos **grupos**.

Nesse momento começo a perguntar para as pessoas o que elas iriam querer em um bar **novo**, qual temática chamaria mais atenção, sabores, nomes, etc.

- Marcela, que tipo de bebidas você gostaria que um bar novo tivesse no **cardápio**? – perguntei para uma amiga que estava em nossa mesa.

- Olha Igor, eu acho que um cardápio mais diversificado de vinhos para serem vendidos individualmente, com uma porção de **queijos** variados, talvez alguns sanduiches leves, isso chamaria a minha atenção.

- Hum, legal. Mas esse bar seria mais **descontraído**, onde as pessoas iriam se encontrar antes de entrarem nas festas. O que acha de cervejas diversas, drinks modernos que tenham uísque com água de coco, destilados pouco conhecidos e salgados (pastel, coxinha, salame, bolinho de mandioca)? – pergunto para Marcela, mas quem responde é sua amiga.

- Acho que não seria um bar com tanta novidade, afinal isso já temos aqui, tem que ser algo onde a pessoa vá para passar pouco tempo, certo? Então deveria **oferecer**, chope bem gelado, cerveja barata, drinks que não demorem e de comida poderia ser fast food, como pizza em pedaços, empadas de sabores pitorescos, **batata frita** de modos diferentes e também pensar no público **vegetariano** ou **vegano** mesmo. – respondeu a Márcia.

- Pode ser, porém não sei se agradaria misturar empada com pizza, será? – perguntei.

- Acho que ficou estranho mesmo, então podia contratar algum chef que faça entradas rápidas e a bebida acho que não tem como inovar tanto, o pessoal gosta mesmo é de cerveja – responde Márcia.

- É uma boa ideia. Posso abrir uma distribuidora e lançar alguns pratos temáticos, isso ficaria a encargo do chef.

Naquele instante meu velho amigo Leo também começa a falar, o cara era um **gênio** da **gastronomia** caseira, fazia maravilhas em casa.

- Caramba, Igor. Tenho ideias fantásticas, já penso em servir pequenos pães de **alho** com **linguiça**, porém com tempero gostoso e harmonizar com cerveja clara ou suco de maracujá. Quem não gosta de nenhum dos dois que beba **refrigerante** mesmo. – disse Leo.

- Nossa, fiquei com água na boca! Tem mais sugestões?

- Muitas, meu amigo.

E assim com muita conversa e **meses** de pesquisa e árduo trabalho, a inauguração do meu bar em parceria com alguns amigos ficou para o dia 10 de março, dia do doce de leite.

Para comemorar e aproveitar a temática lançamos uma sobremesa que levava **sorvete** com muito doce de leite, uma delícia, fora o drink temático, que ficou muito gostoso com a mistura de vodka e licor de doce de leite.

O bar Aurora foi inaugurado com muito **sucesso**; ser popular na faculdade teve suas recompensas, a **notícia** se espalhou depressa e a casa estava cheia. Esse nome foi escolhido por significar o início de qualquer coisa, então lá seria o ponto de partida para qualquer **evento** importante que acontece depois.

Ali pude apreciar grupos de amigos parecidos com os meus, grupo **jovem** que queria colocar o papo em dia e aqueles que quisessem engatavam na **balada**. Alguns já tinham seus pedidos favoritos, como a famosa **barra de cereal** (bacon feito de maneira diferente), pastel de camarão, caldo de mandioquinha, bolinho de bacalhau descontruído e uma seleta opção de hambúrgueres apetitosos.

Com grande êxito, ficamos logo **conhecidos** na cidade, os pratos de comida ganharam notoriedade, nosso drink com amarula fazia o maior sucesso, estávamos sempre com a casa **cheia**. Abríamos a partir das 17 horas e fechávamos às 2 da manhã.

Os **funcionários** chegavam cedo para **organizar** tudo, então antes de iniciar os serviços do dia, eu sempre colocava uma mesa de café da tarde para todos, onde encontravam pão com **manteiga**, leite, café, bolo de milho, tudo para já começarem o trabalho felizes.

Outro fato **curioso** é que a localidade também ficou melhor, as ruas ficaram mais cheias e até o comércio local ficou melhor, outros bares também abriram (nenhum igual ao nosso), assim como alguns food trucks ficavam próximos ao bar. Perto do Aurora só ficava o Macarrão da Dona Neide, como no meu cardápio não tinha essa opção, era liberado que ela ficasse ali, até eu ia lá às vezes comer uma macarronada ou um risoto de alho poró. Também tinham aqueles que **vendiam** churrasquinho, arroz com farofa, uma diversidade grande.

Lembra daquela sugestão de incluir no cardápio opções vegetarianas? Não esqueci delas, um petisco que fazia muito sucesso era o torresmo vegetariano, uma espécie de penne temperado que era frito, uma delícia. Outra coisa que chamava minha atenção era o food truck **inspirado** em Paris, caramba o rapaz conseguia vender macarrons, chocolate quente, crepe com nutella, fazia o maior sucesso.

De repente aquela **rua** se tornou um local de encontro em geral, onde as pessoas tinham opção para tudo, desde algo corriqueiro até lugares para toda a noite. Fiquei muito feliz com todo o acontecimento, não esperava encontrar na abertura de um bar a **motivação** que faltava em minha **vida**.

Um brinde ao bar Aurora!

Resumo da história

Entre vários bares disponíveis na cidade, o bar Aurora é famoso pelas opções que oferece e sempre ganha a clientela que costuma voltar para aproveitar os petiscos da Dona Maria e as bebidas mais pedidas. Boas opções de comida e bebida atraem os grupos de pessoas mais variados. Aquele bar preferido no qual você faz questão de ir.

Summary of the story

Among several bars in the city, the Aurora bar is famous for the options it offers and always wins the clientele, that often returns to enjoy Dona Maria's snacks and the most requested drinks. Good food and drink options attract the most diverse groups of people. It is that favorite bar which you insist on going.

Vocabulary

- **administração:** administration
- **estágio:** internship
- **revolucionária:** revolutionary
- **preocupar:** to worry
- **coquetéis:** cocktails
- **lotado:** crowded
- **cerveja:** beer
- **álcool:** alcohol
- **diversos:** many
- **pedido:** order
- **salame:** salami
- **reunidos:** together
- **ponto de encontro:** meeting point
- **grupos:** groups
- **novo:** new
- **cardápio:** menu
- **queijos:** cheese
- **descontraído:** casual
- **oferecer:** to offer
- **batata frita:** french fries
- **vegetariano:** vegetarian
- **vegano:** vegan
- **gênio:** genius
- **gastronomia:** gastronomy
- **alho:** garlic
- **linguiça:** sausage
- **refrigerante:** soda
- **meses:** months
- **sorvete:** ice cream
- **sucesso:** success
- **notícia:** news
- **evento:** event
- **jovem:** young
- **balada:** night club
- **barra de cereal:** cereal bar
- **conhecidos:** known
- **cheia:** full
- **funcionários:** employees
- **organizar:** to organize
- **manteiga:** butter
- **curioso:** curious
- **vendiam:** sold
- **inspirado:** inspired
- **rua:** street
- **motivação:** motivation
- **vida:** life
- **um brinde:** cheers / a toast

Questions about the story

1. **bar Aurora ficava:**

   a. perto da escola, na Rua Assunção.

   b. perto da esquina, na Rua Conceição.

   c. perto da faculdade, na rua Conceição.

   d. perto da faculdade, na rua Assunção.

2. **Dentre os quitutes de Dona Maria tinha:**

   a. De pizza a hamburguer

   b. de pastéis a picanha com mandioca

   c. de empada a pizza

   d. de mandioca a batata

3. **Márcia sugere que Igor contrate um profissional para fazer:**

   a. entradas rápidas

   b. sanduíches

   c. batata frita

   d. pizza

4. **Márcia sugere que o amigo não inove tanto, pois:**

   a. O pessoal gosta mesmo é de comida.

   b. As pessoas gostam mesmo é de festa.

   c. O pessoal só gosta do tradicional.

   d. As pessoas gostam mesmo é de cerveja.

5. **No bar Aurora, o drink que fez o maior sucesso tinha:**

   a. vodka

   b. cachaça

   c. amarula

   d. alho poró

Anwsers

1. C
2. B
3. A
4. D
5. C

CHAPTER THIRTEEN

PROFESSIONS AND HOBBIES

Momento de decidir a vida! - Time for a life decision!

É chegado o **grande momento** de decidir o que fazer depois de terminar o **colegial**, qual **profissão** seguir, quais **cursos** fazer, mudança de grupos de amigos, mudança de **rotina**, isso tudo com apenas dezessete anos, uma **loucura**! Comecei a **investigar** as profissões e quais seriam as **minhas escolhas** e fui eliminando até chegar em uma só: pensei em ser **médico**, mas aí acompanhei meu tio em seu dia a dia e percebi que não tinha aptidão para carreira de saúde, logo eliminei várias outras como enfermeiro, **dentista**, técnico em laboratório, fisioterapeuta. Realmente a saúde não era a minha **área**, ficava enjoado com qualquer coisa, não dava.

Meu pai era **contador**, passava o dia em cima de números e calculadoras, o que eu não achava ruim, então decidi questioná-lo sobre quando e como ele decidiu ser contador.

- Pai, como, quando, onde, o que aconteceu para que o senhor escolhesse as Ciências Contábeis? – perguntei a ele.

- Ah, filho, essa é muito fácil, sua avó era contadora também, às vezes eu a acompanhava no trabalho e adorava ficar lá, sempre tive muita facilidade com **números** e queria escolher entre contador ou economista, a tarefa foi mais fácil quando conheci um economista e discutindo o que ele fazia percebi que seria mesmo era contador.

E você meu jovem, quais são suas opções? Os vestibulares estão chegando, vai continuar a jogar tênis e fazer **natação** ou se dedicar totalmente aos estudos?

Essas perguntas me deixaram **pensativo**, quase entrei em **pânico**, não tinha uma resposta concreta para dar. Meus hobbies eram importantes para mim, demorei para conseguir gostar desses, já tinha tentado jogar futebol, vôlei, **xadrez** e até aula de dança!

- Estou muito indeciso, o que o senhor acha de ter um filho advogado, ou empresário? – respondi para ele.

- Bom, as duas carreiras parecem promissoras, mas não vejo você sendo nenhuma das duas. Pensei que iria querer ser **veterinário**, gosta tanto de cuidar dos animais, até mesmo dos mais diversos. – disse meu pai.

- Pois é, mas já descartei qualquer profissão relacionada à saúde. Outra carreira que pensei é a de **engenheiro**, acho que seria uma boa escolha, pois gosto de **matemática** e de descobrir coisas novas.

- É interessante mesmo, busque na internet opções para os cursos de engenharia, vou ver se o tio André pode conversar um pouco com você, afinal ele é engenheiro civil.

- Excelente ideia, vou agora mesmo pesquisar; quanto aos hobbies, não irei parar, eles me fazem muito bem. – respondi para meu pai.

Na semana seguinte na minha escola iria acontecer a **feira** de profissões, onde vários profissionais falam sobre suas carreiras e incentivam os alunos com suas histórias e escolhas.

No dia seguinte antes da feira fui conversar com o tio André, o rapaz que era engenheiro, muito amigo de meu pai, tanto que se consideravam irmãos. Eles se conheceram no jogo de carteado que acontecia em nossa **igreja** e também praticavam corrida juntos.

- Olá, João, quer dizer que você quer ser engenheiro? Boa, garoto! Excelente escolha.

- Sim, está na minha lista de **interesses**. Pode contar um pouco mais sobre o seu dia a dia e porque a engenharia civil? Existem tantas outras, como mecânica, ambiental, elétrica, etc.

Nós passamos horas conversando, realmente o trabalho do tio era interessante, trabalhava na parte de **construção civil** em vias urbanas, como construção de **pontes** e via de tráfego, lidava com pedreiros, topógrafos, arquitetos, bem legal! Mas ainda assim, eu estava em dúvida.

Na feira de profissões acabei conhecendo muitas outras profissões, não sabia que existiam tantas! Conversando com um colega percebi que não era o único indeciso.

- João, qual profissão você quer? Queria uma que me levasse para os mais diversos lugares. Estava pensando em ser **piloto**, o que acha? – disse meu amigo, o Zé.

- Caramba, Zé! Você teria coragem, deve ser bom demais! Você ia viajar bastante e ainda ganhar para isso. Ainda não me decidi, estou entre engenharia civil ou área de informática. – respondi ao Zé.

- Eu teria! Minha mãe é **comissária de bordo**, trabalha em uma das maiores companhias do país e ela ama o que faz! Mais do que o seu hobbie por costura. Você chegou a conversar com o analista de sistemas que está naquele banco verde? – disse Zé.

- Ainda não, vou lá agora. Valeu, piloto!

Chegando até a banca verde dou sorte, pois o rapaz estava sozinho e pude conversar bastante com ele sobre como escolheu a carreira de informática. Descobri que existiam diversas **opções**, e que a especialidade dele (analista de sistemas) era apenas uma entre dezenas.

- Na área de informática você pode atuar como desenvolver de softwares, suporte técnico, **programador**, administrator de banco de dados, digitador, e muitas outras. O importante é ter pensamento analítico e gostar de ciências exatas; isso você poderia intensificar jogando xadrez, ou fazendo palavras cruzadas. Claro, as carreiras em informática vão exigir de você muito estudo, mas pode ser bastante recompensador. – respondeu o analista de sistemas.

- Nossa, quanta coisa legal! Deve ser moleza distribuir tanto conhecimento. – respondi ao rapaz.

- Nem tanto, quando terminei a faculdade, ingressei no **mestrado** e logo ao entrar no mercado de trabalho fui chamado para ser professor de uma turma do curso de ciência da computação. Foi bem difícil, sou uma pessoa mais centrada e não conseguia passar o conhecimento adiante da mesma forma como eu executava as tarefas, então deixei de dar aulas, mas a **carreira** de professor também é excelente.

Após conversar por mais de meia hora com o rapaz, decido que precisava acalmar os ânimos e pensar direito.

- Interessante, vou pesquisar mais e agradeço muito seus conselhos. – assim me despedi do rapaz.

- Disponha, meu jovem! E venha ser da informática!

Voltando para casa, percebi que gosto muito de matemática, mas não seria tão bom em chefiar uma equipe como meu tio André; gostava da carreira contábil, porém não me motivava o suficiente.

Ao chegar, conversei com meu pai e minha mãe e cheguei à **conclusão** de que iria fazer seis meses de intercâmbio para aprimorar meu inglês e por enquanto estava decidido a ser analista de sistemas. Ufa, que alívio, toda essa **indecisão** era difícil de suportar.

Resumo da história

Escolher uma profissão nem sempre é algo fácil. João está pensando em sua futura profissão e conversa com familiares e conhecidos para saber mais sobre suas áreas de atuação para finalmente conseguir encontrar uma profissão que tenha a ver com ele.

Summary of the story

Choosing a profession is not always easy. John is thinking about his future profession and talks with his family and acquaintances to know more about their areas of action to finally find a profession that suits him.

Vocabulary

- **grande momento:** big moment
- **colegial:** high school
- **profissão:** profession
- **cursos:** courses
- **rotina:** routine
- **loucura:** madness
- **investigar:** to investigate
- **escolhas:** choices
- **médico:** doctor
- **denstista:** dentist
- **área:** field
- **contatos:** accountant
- **números:** numbers
- **natação:** swimming
- **pensativo:** thoughtful
- **pânico:** panic
- **xadrez:** chess
- **veterinário:** vet
- **engenheiro:** engineer
- **matemática:** math
- **feira:** fair
- **igreja:** church
- **interesses:** interests
- **construção civil:** construction
- **pontes:** bridges
- **piloto:** pilot
- **comissária de bordo:** flight attendant
- **opções:** options
- **programador:** programmer
- **mestrado:** master's
- **carreira:** career
- **conclusão:** conclusion
- **indecisão:** indecision

Questions about the story

1. **Qual foi a primeira escolha profissional pensada?**

   a. dentista
   b. enfermeiro
   c. médico
   d. fisioterapeuta

2. **Qual era a profissão da avó?**

   a. economista
   b. contadora
   c. dentista
   d. advogada

3. **Qual era a profissão do tio?**

   a. engenheiro ambiental
   b. arquiteto
   c. engenheiro civil
   d. topógrafo

4. **Qual é a profissão da mãe de Zé?**

   a. piloto
   b. comissária de bordo
   c. analista de sistemas
   d. desenvolvedora

5. **Após muito pensar, estava decidido em ser:**

   a. médico
   b. engenheiro
   c. professor
   d. analista

Anwsers

1. C
2. B
3. C
4. B
5. D

CHAPTER FOURTEEN

PREPOSITION AND ADVERB OF PLACE

**São nas dificuldades que encontramos amigos -
In the difficulties we find friends**

- João, fui **diagnosticada** com câncer de mama. E agora? – disse minha mãe.

Aquele momento foi tão estarrecedor, minha mãe tinha cinquenta e cinco anos, estava recém **aposentada** e teria uma batalha contra o **câncer** da qual ela teria que **vencer** de qualquer modo. E foi naquele **instante** que soube que eu também teria de lutar pela vida de minha mãe. Então eu a respondi:

- Agora, minha mãe, nós vamos achar o melhor **tratamento** dessa cidade e a senhora será curada. Jamais vou **desistir** de você e você jamais pode desistir de si mesma.

- Obrigada, meu filho, sem você eu não teria **forças** para continuar. – disse minha mãe (Dona Eliana).

No dia seguinte, fui até o médico que a diagnosticou e **conversei** seriamente para saber as **possibilidades** de tratamento, com a companhia de minha mãe, claro.

Ele falou sobre os tratamentos e nos indicou uma **clínica** de sua confiança, ali podíamos confiar que minha mãe seria bem tratada. A clínica indicada ficava próxima de nossa casa, então seria menos **árduo** o trajeto até lá.

Na **segunda-feira** já fui até lá e marquei as primeiras **sessões** de quimioterapia. Ao retornar à casa notei que minha mãe não parava de olhar **fotos** antigas e estava cheia de saudosismo e bastante abatida; por muitos anos não a via daquele jeito. O **livro** que ela mais gostava estava sob a **mesa** junto às fotos, nele tinha um recado **especial** de meu pai, pois foi ele que a presenteou.

Olhando toda aquela cena percebi que precisava trazer alegria para aquela casa, e lembrei que minha irmã ainda não tinha sido informada da situação, então imediatamente peguei o **telefone**, liguei para Luisa e pedi que viesse em casa e **trouxesse** seus filhos.

- Luisa, gostaria de ter uma conversa com você... – disse com um tom que a preocupou.

Para que ela não ficasse tão abatida na frente de nossa mãe, contei por telefone um pouco do que estava acontecendo e de imediato ela se prontificou a aparecer em nossa **casa** na manhã seguinte.

Com a **família** toda reunida, pois éramos somente nós três de adultos e os dois filhos de minha **irmã**, tivemos uma conversa **séria**, confirmamos as datas das sessões de quimioterapia e quem poderia acompanhar Dona Eliana em cada dia lá na clínica. Ela já estava um pouco mais animada, pois avisei na noite anterior que seus **netos** viriam fazer uma visita.

Levantou cedo, fez bolo de chocolate e bolinhos de chuva, tudo para agradar a quem, a mim? Claro que não! Aos netos dela, muito mimados. Mas, foi bom, ela estava mais despreocupada.

Três dias se passaram e é chegada a hora da **primeira** sessão de quimioterapia. Minha mãe havia decidido que não queria **espalhar** a notícia da doença e não iria falar para **ninguém**. Não concordei, mas **respeitei** sua decisão.

- Mãe, a senhora está pronta para seguir adiante? – perguntei para minha mãe ao chegarmos na clínica.

- Sim, aqui será ótimo o tratamento. – ela respondeu segurando um terço que Luísa havia lhe presenteado.

Chegando lá, a recepção era fria, as pessoas na sala de espera estavam sérias e ficavam **analisando** todo o nosso andar. Porém, as moças da **recepção** nos trataram muito bem e em poucos minutos o médico nos chamou.

Dentro do consultório ele fez uma rápida **explicação** do que seria feito naquele dia e nos conduziu para a sala de tratamento, lá, minha mãe iniciou a **medicação**.

Nos dias seguintes minha mãe passou muito mal como **reação** da medicação, mas mesmo assim deu continuidade ao seu tratamento, algumas vezes ia comigo, outras com Luísa, e os netos passaram a fazer mais visitas na tentativa de **alegrar** a vó.

Em uma de suas sessões conhecemos Dona Maria, uma simpática senhora que já estava lutando pela segunda vez contra o câncer, ela e minha mãe se tornaram amigas, trocaram **confidências** e sempre que a encontrávamos, esta senhora tinha o maior zelo por minha mãe.

- Eliana, minha amiga, tenha forças, nós duas vamos nos curar e iremos comemorar tomando sol na praia de Copacabana. Longe dessa clínica e perto do **mar**! – dizia Dona Maria.

Minha mãe sempre respondia:

- Ah, Dona Maria, não vejo a hora de comprarmos as passagens, faz tempo que não vejo o mar! Com certeza iremos passar dias **maravilhosos** por lá.

As duas se tornaram muito amigas. Cantavam pelos corredores da clínica, ambas adoravam Roberto Carlos e faziam diversos **planos** juntas. Me agradava ver minha mãe feliz daquele jeito, apesar de estar em um momento tão difícil.

Em uma de nossas idas para a clínica notei a falta de Dona Maria e fui **questionar** as recepcionistas sobre onde e como ela estava, e, como muita tristeza, me disseram que ela havia falecido. Que choque! Como iria dizer isso para minha mãe?

- Mãe, você terá de ser muito forte agora. Dona Maria não resistiu ao tratamento e **faleceu** ontem, sinto muito!! – disse com muita dor no coração.

Neste momento, minha mãe se atirou sobre meu peito e chorou muito até a sessão de quimioterapia acabar. Ficou com o **coração partido**, ali dentro da sala de recuperação.

Retornamos para casa e notei uma grande tristeza em minha mãe, que começou a falar que achava que também não iria resistir.

Sem que ela soubesse, tomei a decisão de contar para toda família e amigos o que estávamos passando. De repente, **parentes** de longe, perto, amigos que moravam na rua acima e outros que aqui e ali iam se manifestando, começaram a trazer consolo para minha mãe. Suas amigas começaram a fazer **companhia** dia e noite.

- Meu filho, você falou com todas essas pessoas, não imaginava que se importavam tanto comigo! Muito obrigada, mais uma vez você me surpreende positivamente, que alegria. – disse minha mãe, após receber inúmeras manifestações de carinho.

Notei que, apesar da perda de sua amiga, Dona Eliana precisava de forças para continuar e precisava ver que era querida por várias pessoas, além de seus filhos e netos. A tática deu certo, a recuperação foi formidável.

Agora ela sempre tinha com quem conversar e se alegrar, as **rotinas** do tratamento se tornaram mais leves e, sim, ela venceu o câncer e passou a dar mais apoio àqueles que ela sabia que não tinham em quem **confiar**.

Resumo da história

Minha mãe foi diagnosticada com câncer e a partir deste momento nós e nossa família juntamos forças para lutar contra essa doença terrível e entre altos e baixos das sessões de quimioterapia e perdas, a cura e recuperação da doença aconteceram.

Summary of the story

My mother was diagnosed with cancer and from this time we and our family joined forces to fight against this terrible disease and between ups and downs of chemotherapy sessions and losses, healing and recovery from the disease happened.

Vocabulary

- **diagnosticada:** diagnosed
- **aposentada:** retired
- **câncer:** cancer
- **vencer:** to win
- **instante:** moment
- **tratamento:** treatment
- **desistir:** to give up
- **forças:** strengh
- **conversei:** talked
- **possibilidades:** possibilities
- **clínica:** clinic
- **árduo:** difficult
- **segunda-feira:** Monday
- **sessões:** sessions
- **fotos:** pictures
- **livro:** book
- **mesa:** table
- **especial:** special
- **telefone:** telephone
- **trouxesse:** brought
- **casa:** house
- **família:** family
- **irmã:** sister
- **séria:** serious
- **netos:** grandchildren
- **primeira:** first
- **espalhar:** to spread
- **ninguém:** nobody
- **respeitei:** respected
- **analisando:** analysing
- **recepção:** reception
- **explicação:** explanation
- **medicação:** medication
- **reação:** reaction
- **alegrar:** to cheer up
- **confidências:** confidences
- **mar:** sea
- **maravilhosos:** wonderful
- **planos:** plans
- **questionar:** to ask
- **faleceu:** passed away
- **coração partido:** broken heart
- **parentes:** relatives
- **companhia:** company
- **rotinas:** routine
- **confiar:** to trust

Questions about the story

1. **Com que tipo de câncer foi diagnosticada a mãe de João?**

   a. com câncer de pulmão

   b. com câncer de ovário

   c. com câncer de mama

   d. com câncer de pele

2. **A clínica indicada para o tratamento da mãe de João ficava:**
   a. longe da casa deles

   b. perto da casa deles

   c. ao lado da casa deles

   d. em frente à casa deles

3. **João marcou as primeiras sessões de quimioterapia...**

   a. na terça-feira

   b. na quinta-feira

   c. na quarta-feira

   d. na segunda-feira

4. **Quantos adultos tinham na família?**

   a. três adultos e duas crianças

   b. dois adultos e três crianças

   c. quatro adultos e uma criança

   d. dois adultos e duas crianças

5. **Dona Maria dizia que ela e Eliana iriam comemorar tomando sol...**

   a. em Botafogo

   b. em Copacabana

   c. no Leblon

   d. em Ipanema

Anwsers

1. C
2. B
3. D
4. A
5. B

CHAPTER FIFTEEN

PUNCTUATION

Querida gramática! – Dear Grammar!

Prazer, meu nome é Bela. Sou **professora** de português para **crianças** e **adolescentes,** formada relativamente nova, aos vinte e dois anos, na universidade pública mais prestigiada do **país!**

Quando **pequena** achava que me tornando professora estaria sendo uma pessoa completamente realizada. Como crianças não sabem o **futuro** e insistem em achar que ele será **fácil, simples** e **descomplicado,** eu não imaginava os **desafios** que enfrentaria logo no início do exercício da minha profissão.

No ano de minha **formatura** achava que já teria o **emprego** dos sonhos, assim que saísse da faculdade; "doce" engano, as dificuldades só estavam começando. Como minha **mãe** dizia: "essa menina está sempre no mundo da lua".

Ao terminar a **graduação** resolvi prestar **concurso** para **lecionar** na rede pública do estado, logo fui **aprovada** e convocada, fui **alocada** em uma das escolas com pior índice de **rendimento** e sem muita perspectiva de melhoria. O colégio tinha como **necessidade** bons professores para o ensino básico, então fui escolhida para esta tarefa, e durante dois anos lecionei para crianças e uma das suas maiores dificuldades era a **pontuação.**

Como **tentativa** de chamar a atenção dessas crianças e de repassar o conteúdo de modo eficiente comecei a criar **histórias** onde os símbolos de pontuação explicavam sua própria **importância**. Para tentar ajudar outros professores, vou mostrar um trecho dos "Magníficos Pontos de Vista em A tarefa mais difícil".

"Os **sinais** de pontuação não conseguiam mais **dormir** dentro do **livro** mais temido de todos, o livro de Gramática, tudo isso porque estavam se sentido sem importância, **incompreendidos**. Mas tem sempre um tagarela para iniciar uma discussão e Dona **Vírgula** se pronunciou:

– Ai, ai, tem algum **erro** nessa história – disse a Vírgula.

– Como assim, vírgula? – perguntou "o indeciso", o Ponto de **Interrogação**.

– As **pessoas** não sabem que devo estar sempre presente para **separar** frases desencadeadas entre si ou **elementos** dentro de uma frase?

– **Lógico!!** Concordo com você! – disse "o autoritário", o Ponto de **Exclamação**.

– Entenderam a minha importância? – disse a Virgula.

Nessa hora todos acordaram e começou a **discussão**.

– Eu também sou importante. – gritou o **Travessão.** – Se não fosse por mim o **leitor** não saberia que era você que estava falando.

– Nós também! – disseram as **Aspas**. Somos **ótimos** para chamar atenção para algo, chamar atenção é com a gente, só chamar.

– Pode me **incluir** também, sempre presente antes das Aspas e do Travessão. – comentou o Dois Pontos.

– Somos o **exército** da boa **escrita!** Como missão devemos dar **clareza** aos **textos;** se nos confundirem, vira uma confusão! – disse glamoroso, o Ponto de Exclamação.

– Concordo, se nos colocam de maneira errada, podemos alterar todo o **sentido** de uma frase ou dar **margem** para outras interpretações... – apareceu a Senhora **Reticências.**

– Sim, uma pontuação errada muda tudo. – disse o Ponto Final, sempre presente.

– Se eu aparecer depois da frase "acha que sabe tudo" – disse o Ponto de Interrogação – é apenas uma pergunta, certo?

– Mas se **eu** aparecer é como se fosse uma **certeza.** – disse a Exclamação - "Acha que sabe tudo!"

– Estamos na área! – riram as Aspas.

– Eu estive sempre aí, desde o **início.** – disse o Travessão.

– Para evitar **mal-entendido** não basta um **ponto,** nem vírgula, são necessários os dois. – disse o tímido Ponto e Vírgula.

– Melhor mesmo é quando nos chamam para fazer um texto corretinho. – disse a Vírgula.

– Então devem nos usar **corretamente!** – gritou o Ponto Final.

Fim da discussão."

Voltei! Observaram como ficou mais **suave** o **aprendizado?**

Essas histórias melhoraram **significativamente** o entendimento dos **alunos,** o interesse também aumentou, pois queriam usar corretamente as pontuações. Nós, como professores, temos o dever de **explicar** quantas vezes forem necessárias para que o aluno entenda, muitas vezes isso demanda tempo e criatividade.

No colégio que estava falando anteriormente os índices elevaram após uma boa **recauchutada** na forma como as crianças eram ensinadas; muitas só iam para o colégio para ter o que **comer,** outras para escapar da **realidade** de suas casas, mas poucas com o real interesse de aprender algo **novo.**

O próprio **diretor** que estava ali há muitos anos no comando de todo o **colégio** observou a melhoria e o interesse de muitos alunos, com isso muitos professores vieram até minha sala e pediram **ajuda** para também melhorarem suas **táticas** de ensino. Confesso, fiquei muito **surpresa**, mas aquela menininha que sonhava em ser professora com certeza estava muito feliz. Nessas **horas** percebo que escolhi a profissão correta. A arte de fazer a diferença é muito prazerosa!

Um dia "peguei" minha mãe falando com uma conhecida sobre mim: "Nossa, a Bela está tão feliz em seu emprego novo! Acho que ela está fazendo um belo trabalho, escolhi o nome certo para essa minha menininha."

O ensino básico deve ser tratado com muito carinho, veja bem, se uma criança desde muito pequena fosse incentivada a ler vários livros e recompensada por fazer seus deveres de **casa** ou mesmo se alguém apontasse sempre suas **evoluções**, com toda certeza nossos **problemas sociais** seriam bem menores do que são hoje.

Em uma **breve** conversa com o professor de história pude ajudá-lo a melhorar suas aulas, recordo-me como se fosse hoje.

- Professora Bela, tudo bem? Venho observando a melhora na escrita de meus alunos, acredito que sejam suas aulas fazendo **efeito**! Tem alguma **dica** para que eu possa melhorar as minhas? – disse Roberto, o Professor de História.

- Claro, vamos ver. Roberto você já tentou introduzir o teatro em suas aulas? Como acha que os alunos se sairiam se fossem encorajados a representar os personagens históricos, iam ter que estudar sobre eles, certo? E a **introdução** de novos **livros, filmes** curtos? A história só teria a ganhar com essas táticas, não acha? – respondi ao professor.

- Nossa, Bela! Adorei suas dicas, vou pôr essas táticas em ação e te mantenho informada.

Resultado: Após algumas semanas recebi um convite para assistir à apresentação dos alunos sobre História do Brasil. A peça foi ótima, estavam todos super engajados e confiantes, recebi até um agradecimento ao final do espetáculo. **Orgulho** que não cabe em mim! E pretendo fazer muitas outras ações! Educação não é despesa e sim investimento. Se as pessoas pensassem dessa **maneira**...

Resumo da história

Uma professora cria histórias para ensinar aos seus alunos sobre gramática e, percebendo que os estudantes tinham muita dificuldade sobre pontuação, resolve escrever uma história dando ênfase neste tema.

Summary of the story

A teacher creates stories to teach grammar to her students and realizing that they had great difficulty in punctuation, she decides to write a story with an emphasis on this topic.

Vocabulary

- **prazer:** pleasure
- **professora:** teacher
- **crianças:** kids
- **adolescentes:** teenagers
- **país:** country
- **pequena:** young
- **futuro:** future
- **fácil:** easy
- **simples:** simple
- **descomplicado:** uncomplicated
- **desafios:** challenges
- **formatura:** graduation
- **emprego:** job
- **mãe:** mother
- **graduação:** graduation
- **concurso:** test/application (for a job)
- **lecionar:** to teach
- **aprovada:** approved
- **alocada:** allocated
- **rendimento:** productivity
- **necessidade:** necessity
- **pontuação:** grade
- **tentativa:** attempt
- **histórias:** stories
- **importância:** importance

- **sinais:** signs
- **dormir:** to sleep
- **livro:** book
- **incompreendidos:** misunderstood
- **vírgula:** comma
- **erro:** mistake
- **interrogação:** interrogation point
- **pessoas:** people
- **separar:** to divide
- **elementos:** elements
- **lógico:** of course
- **exclamação:** exclamation point
- **discussão:** argument
- **travessão:** crossing
- **aspas:** quotation marks
- **ótimos:** great
- **incluir:** to include
- **exército:** army
- **escrita:** writing
- **clareza:** clarity
- **textos:** texts
- **sentido:** sense
- **margem:** margin
- **reticências:** suspension points

- **eu:** I / me
- **certeza:** assurance
- **início:** beginning
- **mal-entendido:** misunderstanding
- **ponto:** point
- **corretamente:** correctly
- **fim:** end
- **suave:** smooth
- **aprendizado:** learning
- **significativamente:** significantly
- **alunos:** students
- **explicar:** to explain
- **recauchutada:** retreaded
- **comer:** to eat
- **realidade:** reality
- **novo:** new

- **diretor:** director
- **colégio:** high school
- **ajuda:** help
- **táticas:** tactics
- **surpresa:** surprise
- **horas:** hours
- **casa:** house
- **evoluções:** evolutions
- **problemas sociais:** social problems
- **breve:** short
- **efeito:** effect
- **dica:** tip
- **introdução:** introduction
- **livros:** books
- **filmes:** movies
- **orgulho:** proud
- **maneira:** way

Questions about the story

1. **Qual pontuação disse que havia um erro na história?**

    a. o ponto de interrogação

    b. o ponto-e-vírgula

    c. a vírgula

    d. o ponto final

2. **Qual pontuação era autoritária?**

    a. o ponto de exclamação

    b. o ponto de interrogação

    c. o ponto final

    d. a vírgula

3. **Qual pontuação serve para chamar a atenção?**

    a. o ponto final

    b. o ponto-e-vírgula

    c. o travessão

    d. as aspas

4. **Qual pontuação está sempre presente entre as aspas e o travessão?**

    a. a vírgula

    b. os dois pontos

    c. o ponto-e-vírgula

    d. o ponto final

5. **Qual pontuação serve para introduzir falas?**

    a. o travessão

    b. o ponto-e-vírgula

    c. o ponto final

    d. os dois pontos

Answers

1. C
2. A
3. D
4. B
5. A

CHAPTER SIXTEEN

VERBS IN GERUND

Provas no colégio - Exams at school

Quando estavam **chegando** as **primeiras** provas no **colégio** daquele ano de 2015, lembro da sensação de desespero, pois eu não estava **estudando** como deveria! Estava **cursando** o **último** ano do ensino médio e **mudando** meu comportamento no colégio para tentar alcançar médias maiores, já que as universidades que gostaria de entrar eram bastante concorridas.

Resolvi pedir ajudar a minha **melhor** amiga, Silvia, pois era muito inteligente e vivia estudando pelos cantos do colégio; a **pessoa** certa e que adoraria me **ajudar**.

- Silvinha, vamos **estudar** lá em casa para as provas da semana? Estou **precisando** de ajuda, por favor.

- É claro, Maria. Já estava **notando** sua falta de **atenção** nas aulas, principalmente as de matemática. Está **acontecendo** alguma coisa?

- Ando muito cansada, esse ano decidi fazer estágio após a escola para ajudar em casa, e estou **trabalhando** muito. – respondi para Silvia.

- Realmente, trabalhar todos os **dias** e ainda ter ânimo para continuar estudando fica difícil, mas como faremos então?

- Eu pedi essa semana de férias, não estaria **rendendo** nada em nenhum dos dois, tanto no colégio quanto no trabalho se estivesse preocupada com as provas como estou. Os chefes da minha diretoria acabaram me **liberando**, eles são compreensivos.

- **Entendo**, que bom! Vou até a sua **casa** depois do **almoço**, certo?

- Sim, muito **obrigada** Silvinha. – Respondi. Estava aliviada porque ela aceitou me ajudar.

Após o colégio fui direto para casa e arrumei tudo para receber minha **amiga.** Confesso que estava até feliz de estar me **esforçando** para as provas, isso nunca havia acontecido.

Logo por volta das duas da tarde começamos os estudos. Primeiro estudamos **matemática**, pois o meu conhecimento nessa disciplina era horrível, fico **anotando** tudo do quadro, mas quando vou fazer algum exercício simplesmente não consigo. Silvia achou minha dificuldade e me deu algumas dicas para ir **focando** e **resolvendo** de uma vez por todas.

Depois mudamos de assunto, começamos a estudar **história**. Nessa hora me surpreendi, quem estava **ajudando** mais era eu! Finalmente aquele seriado de época que assistia toda tarde estava sendo útil, estava **morrendo** de rir com essa situação.

Após dois dias do início dos estudos, chegou a hora da primeira **prova**, a de **geografia**.

- Então Maria, está confiante? Está **lembrando** do que estudamos? – perguntou Silvinha.

- Estou sim, estou **confiando** em mim mesma. Vamos arrasar Silvinha!

O **professor** começa a distribuir as provas e eu estava tranquila até receber a minha folha de questões. **Observando** as perguntas percebo que sei responder todas, fico muito feliz, mas preciso **respirar** fundo para **responder** corretamente.

Vou respondendo as questões e de repente percebo uma espécie de choro ao meu lado; era o Marquinhos que não estava **escrevendo** nada e parecia perdido. Depois da prova era **horário** do intervalo e resolvo ir até ele, queria saber o que estava acontecendo.

- Ei, Marquinhos, está tudo bem? Vi que estava **chorando** na prova de geografia, o que houve? – pergunto para ele.

- Maria, eu não sabia responder **nada**, estava me desesperando naquele momento que você me viu. Não consegui estudar nada, não sei o que houve. Não fui bem nesta prova. – Marcos respondeu.

- Calma Marcos, por que não está estudando? Se quiser pode se juntar ao meu grupo **fantástico** de estudos! Tudo bem que ele é composto somente por mim e Silvinha, mas estaremos te **ajudando**, topa?

- Nossa, sério? Como? Quando? Onde? Sim, aceito, estou precisando muito de ajuda. – Marcos responde super empolgado.

- Na minha casa por volta das duas horas da tarde, estamos estudando para as provas, aparece lá hoje. – respondi para ele.

- **Combinado**! – responde Marcos.

Naquela hora percebi que não era somente eu que estava precisando de ajuda, todos temos nossas dificuldades. Vou tentar encontrar Silvinha para contar as novidades. Sei que existe um clima de romance entre esses dois.

No período da tarde nos encontramos todos em minha casa e começamos os estudos. Cada um expôs suas dificuldades; as de Marcos eram muitas, mas daríamos um jeito; Silvia como sempre ajudando mais que tudo. Acho que ela se tornará professora, o que será ótimo.

Com os dias foram passando, os estudos avançando e minhas notas realmente melhorando fui conversar com minha mãe, pois havia decidido sair do estágio que estava fazendo. Para o meu espanto, ela concordou de imediato e disse que estava notando o meu esforço para ter notas melhores. Acredito que assim posso me dedicar ao máximo e realmente conseguir meus **objetivos**, que são audaciosos.

Nossos encontros eram intensificados em **semanas** de provas, mas sempre nos encontrávamos umas **três** vezes na semana para manter os estudos em dia e não ficar nos **sufocando** nas últimas horas antes das provas.

As notas de Marcos estavam bem melhores e ele estava até mais **relaxado** e menos **estressado** com o colégio. As vezes as dificuldades podem surgir e se não pedirmos ajuda pode ser difícil melhorar. Silvia também mudou, estava mais alegre, conversando mais e até a vaidade estava aumentando, afinal se encontrava com Marcos várias vezes na semana e queria estar sempre **bonita**.

E eu? Estava **feliz** da vida, minhas notas estavam **crescendo**, tinha as tardes **livres** para estudar e segui intensificando o curso de inglês. Nosso trio era imbatível, éramos os melhores alunos da classe, mas éramos legais também, não perdemos nada do colégio por conta dos estudos.

Com as datas dos vestibulares chegando, o colégio decidiu investir em simulados para ajudar os estudantes. Achei a ideia ótima, já estava querendo fazer alguns pela internet, ao todo seriam quatro simulados até o final do ano, todos com questões semelhantes às de grandes **universidades**.

Nos dois primeiros, nosso trio não foi muito bem, estávamos estudando com foco nas provas do colégio e esquecemos que no vestibular seriam todas as matérias de uma só vez. Foi então que procuramos ajuda. Lembra que sem ajuda não vamos a lugar nenhum? Pois bem, nossa coordenadora nos atendeu com muito gentileza e nos ajudou a montar um **plano de estudos** focado no vestibular, mas que não iria dificultar nos estudos para as provas do colégio.

Começamos então a seguir este plano e adivinhe só? Melhoramos muito nossas notas no simulado seguinte, estava me **alegrando** muito. Os estudos foram **ficando** intensos, as temidas provas finais foram chegando e os vestibulares viriam logo em seguida, mas decidimos não enlouquecer com tantas coisas para fazer.

As provas do colégio passaram e todos fomos bem nos resultados, comecei a me preocupar somente com o vestibular. Logo no final do ano já tinha um para fazer, de uma universidade **próxima** de minha casa. Queria muito passar nessa prova. Fiz mais duas provas de outras faculdades, e passei nas três. Estava radiante! Silvia e Marcos também foram **aprovados** e não precisaríamos fazer cursinho no ano seguinte.

Acabamos nos separando, pois escolhemos universidades diferentes, mas nunca deixamos de ser amigos. Ah, os dois começaram a **namorar** no ano seguinte, demorou, mas finalmente aconteceu. Foi um ano muito prazeroso, onde consegui definir metas e ter a virtude de continuar sempre **correndo** atrás de todas elas. Tudo deu certo.

Resumo da história

Maria está buscando ajuda para conseguir estudar melhor para as provas da escola, pois está no último ano do ensino médio e em breve irá cursar alguma faculdade. Com a ajuda de seus amigos Silvia e Marcos, ela está pronta para alcançar seus objetivos.

Summary of the story

Maria is seeking help to be able to study better for the school exams, since she is in the final year of high school and will soon go to college. With the help of her friends Silvia and Marcos, she is ready to achieve her goals.

Vocabulary

- **chegando:** arriving
- **primeiras:** first
- **colégio:** high school
- **estudando:** studying
- **cursando:** attending
- **último:** last
- **mudando:** moving
- **melhor:** best
- **pessoa:** person
- **ajudar:** to help
- **estudar:** to study
- **precisando:** needing
- **notando:** noticing
- **atenção:** attention
- **acontecendo:** happening
- **trabalhando:** working
- **dias:** days
- **rendendo:** being efficient
- **liberando:** freeing
- **entendo:** understand
- **casa:** house
- **almoço:** lunch
- **obrigada:** thank you
- **amiga:** friend
- **esforçando:** making an effort
- **matemática:** math
- **anotando:** taking notes
- **focando:** focusing
- **resolvendo:** solving
- **história:** history
- **ajudando:** helping
- **morrendo:** dying
- **prova:** test
- **geografia:** geography
- **lembrando:** remembering
- **confiando:** trusting
- **professor:** teacher
- **observando:** observing
- **respirar:** to breath
- **responder:** to answer
- **escrevendo:** writing
- **horário:** time
- **chorando:** crying
- **nada:** nothing
- **fantástico:** fantastic
- **ajudando:** helping
- **combinado:** deal
- **encontrar:** to meet
- **objetivos:** goals
- **semanas:** weeks
- **três:** three
- **sufocando:** suffocating
- **relaxado:** relaxed
- **estressado:** stressed

- **bonita:** beautiful
- **feliz:** happy
- **crescendo:** growing
- **livre:** free
- **universidades:** universities
- **plano de estudos:** study plan
- **alegrando:** rejoicing
- **ficando:** getting
- **próxima:** close/next
- **aprovados:** approved
- **namorar:** to date
- **correndo:** running

Questions about the story

1. A amiga de Maria, Silvia, vivia _____ pelos cantos.

    a. mudando
    b. chegando
    c. precisando
    d. estudando

2. Maria estava indo mal no colégio e estava _____ da ajuda de Silvia.

    a. precisando
    b. notando
    c. estudando
    d. cursando

3. Marcos estava chorando porque:

    a. sabia toda a matéria da prova
    b. não conseguiu estudar nada
    c. Maria tirou uma nota melhor
    d. estava escrevendo tudo

4. Maria decide sair do estágio e sua mãe:

    a. descordou
    b. reclamou
    c. concordou
    d. notou

5. Silvia e Marcos começaram a namorar:

    a. dois anos depois
    b. no mesmo ano
    c. três anos depois
    d. um ano depois

Answers

1. D
2. A
3. B
4. C
5. D

CHAPTER SEVENTEEN

FUTURE TENSE

Subir ao altar - Climb the altar

Era **primavera** em minha **cidade** e as **flores** estavam lindas e radiantes, os negócios com a confeitaria iam bem, meus pais estavam aposentados e felizes, minha casa estava ficando pronta e meu **cachorro** (Rufus) estava mais **fofo** do que nunca. A única coisa que me preocupava era que eu já estava com trinta e cinco anos e meu namorado (Mário) não me pedia em **casamento**.

Tudo estava indo bem, mas os bons anos de namoro não saíam do status de namoro. Decidi procurar a Paula, minha amiga de longa data, para receber alguns **conselhos**.

- Boa noite, Paula! Obrigada por me receber, as coisas estão ficando **tensas** entre o Mário e eu. – Chego reclamando.

- Eita, Júlia, vamos entrar e **conversar** sobre isso. Veremos o que podemos fazer.

- Minha amiga, o que posso fazer? Eu ouvirei tudo que você tem a dizer. Mário não **demonstra** nada, parece que está tentando **fugir** do assunto. Com onze anos de namoro acho que já é tempo **suficiente**. Quando escutar dele que quer se casar comigo, entrarei em choque. – falei para Paula.

- Julinha, será **especial** e surpreendente quando ele falar, não acha? Com tantos anos de namoro o bom é que você já pôde averiguar se ele é o rapaz certo. Ele é o rapaz certo?

- É ele, todos os dias vou dormir pensando nele, Rufus adora sua companhia, estou planejando toda a **reforma** da casa com o pensamento de nós vivermos para sempre lá. Desde de que nos conhecemos, há muitos anos, minha **admiração** por ele é grande; o que realmente me incomoda é essa **lerdeza** em oficializar as coisas. – respondi para Paulinha.

No meio tempo decidimos sentar do lado de fora da casa e aproveitar o **ar fresco** que estava por vir, também havia levado cookies e uma **torta de morango**, e Paula logo providenciou taças com um bom **vinho**.

- Sabe Júlia, quando casei com o Roberto foi tudo muito corrido e **cedo**, afinal já estava **grávida** de Maria. Hoje vivemos brigando e discutindo, às vezes acho que casei por **impulso** e que como éramos jovens, a falta de curtir a juventude está nos causando problemas. Mas, gosto muito do meu marido e não tenho do que me queixar, é um ótimo pai e bom amigo, decidimos tentar fazer as coisas darem certo. No caso do Mário, ele pode achar que do que jeito que vocês estão não precisa **mudar**. Já tentou falar com ele sobre isso?

- Todo santo dia! Já estou sendo a chata do namoro, por muitas vezes fico emburrada e ele não percebe nada ou finge que não **percebe**. Se Mário obtiver o cargo que almeja na empresa, pode ser que ele **finalmente** faça o pedido. Mas estou cansada de esperar. – respondi.

Acabamos com duas garrafas de vinho e todos os **doces**, fiquei até muito tarde na casa de Paula até seu marido chegar do plantão (Roberto era enfermeiro). Na hora de ir para casa decidirei que tipo de conversa ter com Mário.

Ficarei surpresa se ele tiver me ligado, pois esqueci o celular na confeitaria e só irei buscar no outro dia. Estava tão **chateada** que não lembrei de buscar o celular, pois só queria descansar e ficar com meu cachorro.

No dia seguinte percebo que tenho que **fazer compras** para a loja, existem diversos ingredientes em falta. Vou até a vendedora da loja e digo que irei ao mercado na cidade vizinha, lá a variedade de produtos era maior.

Ao chegar ao mercado encontro uma famosa dona de uma outra confeitaria da cidade, muito educada, ela vem me **cumprimentar**.

- Olá, Júlia, como está você? E a confeitaria? Recebi uma encomenda enorme de seu marido ontem à noite. Vai ter uma grande festa, hein!

Nessa hora fico até gelada, não consigo entender porque Mário estava fazendo aquilo. Deve ser para o meu **aniversário** mês que vem, então vou fingir que sei de tudo.

- Oi, Margarida, tudo bem e com você? Nossa, é mesmo havia me esquecido desse pedido. Mário é meu namorado, ainda não somos casados, mas fico agradecida por ter aceitado o pedido.

- Sem problemas, todos aqueles bem-casados estarão devidamente prontos na data certinha. Tchau, tchau!

Meus Deus! Márcio **encomendou** bem-casados? Como assim? Será que é para agora? Fico chocada nesse momento decido contar para Paula. Que infelizmente estava muito ocupada e não pode me atender. Então decido sondar Márcio sobre esse pedido misterioso.

Adivinhem? Ele acaba revelando que os pedidos foram para o casamento de um amigo que não queria pedir em minha confeitaria para que eu fosse até a festa sem estar cansada do trabalho. Nossa, queria matar o meu **namorado**!!

Naquele mesmo dia resolvi procurar minha mãe para conversar, pois estava agoniada com a situação. Não tinha ninguém em casa, resolvo ligar e minha mãe diz estar muito **ocupada**, ao fundo escuto uma moça dizer: "Senhora, experimente este aqui acho que ficará melhor."

Acho tudo muito estranho, mas decido que vou **trabalhar** até mais tarde para não pensar mais nisso.

No dia seguinte, recebo uma ligação da Paula logo cedo, muito feliz ela diz que ganhou uma promoção de uma loja de roupas e que pode levar uma amiga para escolherem vestidos de graça.

- Opa, como assim vestidos de graça? Que horas você passará para **me buscar**? – respondi para ela.

- Daqui a meia hora buzinarei em sua porta, fique pronta! – Paula responde toda empolgada.

Chegamos em uma das lojas mais famosas da cidade e começamos a **experimentar** alguns vestidos, Paula logo escolhe o dela, um vestido azul muito bonito. Eu fico em dúvida entre dois, mas minha amiga traz uma terceira opção de cair o queixo. Um vestido rosa claro bem brilhante, lindo, lindo.

- Onde você achou este vestido? É lindíssimo. – falo alto perto de Paula.

- Acho que ele estava te esperando esse tempo todo. Vai lá experimentar. – disse Paula.

Aquele vestido era tão lindo, resolvo ficar com ele, na hora de vestir minha **calça** percebo que a mesma está rasgada, será que eu tinha ido até a loja com a calça **rasgada**? Que vergonha! Paula então sugere que eu vá usando o vestido até a confeitaria, onde sempre deixo algumas roupas guardadas para caso precise, e me **troque** lá.

- Tudo bem, irei com esse lindo vestido para minha loja. – respondi para Paula.

Ao chegarmos próximos da loja, percebo uma movimentação estranha, mas continuo o **percurso**, Paula decide descer para comprar alguns **biscoitos** para sua filha, percebo também que ela não tirou o vestido azul.

Cheguei na loja e vi o Rufus todo arrumadinho, lá dentro meus pais todos bem vestidos e arrumados e os funcionários da loja **rindo** pelos cantos, sem entender nada entro na loja e pergunto a todos.

- Pessoal, o que está acontecendo?

- Minha menina, está muito linda... – disse meu pai.

De repente, Mário sai da **cozinha** da confeitaria e está de **terno**, lindo e eu continuo sem entender nada. Ao se aproximar de mim, ele se ajoelha e começa a dizer as coisas mais belas que eu gostaria de ouvir.

- Querida Júlia, a coisa mais **importante** de minha vida. Neste momento estou aqui aos seus pés, diante de todos para pedir sua mão em casamento. **Quer casar comigo?** - disse Mário.

Nessa hora, **desmaiei**.

Mas acordei logo e disse sim mil vezes. Que emoção foi aquele momento e todos já sabiam do pedido e não me contaram nada. Os bem-casados? Estavam lá para a celebração, onde vários amigos começaram a chegar e a nos cumprimentar.

Finalmente, sou **noiva** do Mario!

Resumo da história

Paula estava com a vida toda encaminhada, o trabalho ia bem, seus pais aposentados, seu cachorro lhe fazia companhia e estava muito feliz, mas o único problema que a incomodava era que Mário, seu namorado, não a pedia em casamento. Será que Mário vai perceber o desejo de Paula?

Summary of the story

Paula had her life on the track, work was going well, her parents retired, her dog kept her company and she was very happy, but the only problem that bothered her was that her boyfriend Mario did not ask her to marry him. Will Mario realize the desire of Paula?

Vocabulary

- **primavera:** spring
- **cidade:** city
- **flores:** flowers
- **cachorro:** dog
- **fofo:** cute
- **casamento:** marriage
- **conselhos:** advices
- **tensas:** tense
- **conversar:** to talk
- **demonstra:** show
- **fugir:** to run away
- **suficiente:** enough
- **especial:** special
- **reforma:** renovation
- **admiração:** admiration
- **lerdeza:** sloppiness
- **ar fresco:** fresh air
- **torta de morango:** strawberry pie
- **vinho:** wine
- **cedo:** early
- **grávida:** pregnant
- **impulso:** impulse
- **mudar:** to change
- **percebe:** realize
- **finalmente:** finally
- **doces:** candies
- **chateada:** upset
- **fazer compras:** to go shopping
- **cumprimentar:** to greet
- **aniversário:** birthday
- **encomendou:** ordered
- **adivinhem:** guess what?
- **namorado:** boyfriend
- **ocupada:** busy
- **trabalhar:** to work
- **me buscar:** pick me up
- **experimentar:** to try out
- **calça:** pants
- **rasgada:** torn
- **troque:** change
- **percurso:** way
- **biscoitos:** cookies
- **rindo:** laughing
- **cozinha:** kitchen
- **terno:** suit
- **importante:** important
- **quer casar comigo?:** will you marry me?
- **desmaiei:** fainted
- **noiva:** fiancé

Questions about the story

1. **Julia vai encontrar Paula e leva:**

    a. torta de morango e cookies
    b. cookies e bolo de maçã
    c. torta de morango e pão de queijo
    d. torta de morango e panqueca

2. **Qual é o nome do cachorro de Paula?**

    a. Crucius
    b. Lucius
    c. Brucis
    d. Rufus

3. **Como Paula sabe que Mário é o rapaz certo?**

    a. porque ele faz tudo que ela quer
    b. porque ele não para de pensar nela
    c. porque ela vai dormir pensando nele
    d. Rufus não gosta dele

4. **A calça de Paula rasgou, o que Julia sugere que ela faça?**

    a. Vá com a calça rasgada mesmo
    b. Vá com o vestido novo até a loja
    c. Compre uma nova calça
    d. Vá de calça e troque o vestido na loja

5. **O que Mário diz a Paula?**

    a. As coisas mais belas que ela gostaria de ouvir
    b. As coisas mais absurdas que ela não gostaria de ouvir
    c. Minha menina, está muito linda...
    d. Pessoal, o que está acontecendo?

Answers

1. A
2. D
3. C
4. B
5. A

CHAPTER EIGHTEEN

DAY-TO-DAY TASKS

Essa família é muito unida - This family is very close

Na minha casa **moram** cinco pessoas, eu (Jorge), minha irmã (Carla), meu **irmão** (Silvio) que é **gêmeo** de Carla e meus pais (Dona Maria e Sr. José). Nossa residência é bem simples, mas todos temos nossos quartos e três **banheiros**, fora a área do **quintal** que é a casa do Totó, nosso cachorrinho sem raça que resgatamos aqui na rua debaixo.

Por termos essa casa grande e minha mãe ter problemas no **joelho**, todas as tarefas de casa são divididas entre todos até mesmo com nosso cachorro, que é o segurança da casa. Eu sou o responsável por colocar o lixo na **lixeira** todos os dias às cinco da tarde, pois o caminhão passa para recolhê-lo às cinco e meia, além de lavar um dos banheiros a cada três dias e varrer o quintal sempre que preciso. Meus irmãos têm **tarefas** parecidas, como são gêmeos não se desgrudam, lavam os outros banheiros e a louça suja todas as noites.

Meus pais se dividem no restante das tarefas, eles são muito unidos, tenho um orgulho imenso dos dois. Meu pai é administrador e minha mãe professora de inglês. Eles trabalham de segunda a sexta, mas minha mãe tem horários mais **flexíveis**.

Para demonstrar vou contar como se passa um dia na minha casa.

Acordo às seis e meia da manhã, vou **tomar banho**, **me vestir** para o colégio e desço para o **café da manhã**. Começo a fazer um **suco de laranja** e esquentar uns pães de queijo para todos.

Nesse momento meus irmãos começam a acordar e a discussão já se inicia, um quer tomar banho primeiro que o outro. Quando já estamos todos prontos para irmos ao colégio, meus pais também já estão prontos para irem ao trabalho. Ah, antes de sairmos coloco ração e água para Totó, que ainda está dormindo (muito preguiçoso, esqueci-me de mencionar).

Eu costumo ir ao colégio com minha mãe, e meus irmãos com meu pai. Estudamos em colégios diferentes, sou o mais velho dos três. **Sempre** me despeço do mesmo modo dela.

- Tchau, mãe. Tenha um ótimo dia. – digo.

- Boa aula, filhão! **Preste atenção** nos professores. – ela responde.

Minhas aulas terminam ao meio dia e pego um **ônibus** em frente ao colégio para ir para casa. O trajeto é rápido, mas sempre chego com muita fome.

Toda a quarta vai uma moça fazer uma faxina completa em nossa casa, ela **lava roupa**, passa essas roupas, lava os banheiros, limpa o quintal e os quartos, **passa aspirador** no sofá e o mais importante: faz comida!

- Oi, Josefa, como vai? O almoço está pronto? Estou com muita fome. – digo para ela.

- Oi menino, tudo certo. A comida vai ficar pronta em cinco minutos, vá lavar as mãos e desce para comer.

Vou correndo **lavar as mãos** e desço para comer. Lá de cima consigo sentir o cheiro da comida maravilhosa de Dona Josefa, com certeza ela fez bife com batatas!!

- Será que meu olfato está certo, temos **bife** com batatas para o almoço? – pergunto para ela.

- Acertou quase tudo, pois ainda tem um sorvete de limão para sobremesa. – Josefa me responde morrendo de rir.

Logo após o almoço, que estava delicioso, decido que é hora de fazer o **dever de casa.** Hoje tenho muitos exercícios para praticar. Sento-me em minha escrivaninha e começo pela matemática. Alguns exercícios não consigo resolver sozinho e decido pedir ajuda ao meu pai assim que ele chegar.

Lá do quarto escuto o pessoal da rua me chamando para brincar, mais precisamente **jogar bola.** Peço permissão para a Josefa, que nessa hora estava lavando roupas e que disse que depois iria limpar o chão da sala.

- Josefa, posso jogar bola com os meninos da rua? – pergunto para ela.

- As suas lições do colégio estão feitas? – Josefa questiona.

- Olha, tenho algumas que estão em branco, mas preciso da ajuda de meu pai para fazer. Logo que ele chegar eu peço ajuda. Ok?

- Bom, então pode ir, tome cuidado, você não pode se machucar igual àquela vez. – disse Josefa.

Ela está se referindo ao mês passado quando torci o pé no **futebol** e fiquei todo machucado, passei semanas sem realizar as tarefas de casa. Ela autoriza e então calço minhas chuteiras e vou ao encontro de meus amigos.

Quando chego ao campinho ao lado de minha casa os times já estão até formados e estou escalado como atacante no time do Jairzinho. Fico por mais de duas horas **brincando**, até que começa a escurecer e decido voltar para casa.

Volto **sujo** e cansado para casa, como tinha muita lama no campo, minha chuteira voltou toda enlameada, então vou até o tanquinho e começo a lavar meus sapatos que estavam ali próximos, deixo todos no varal para secar.

Entro em casa e minha mãe já manda aos gritos que eu vá tomar banho, afinal estou muito fedido.

- Jorge, para o **chuveiro** agora!!!! – minha mãe gritou.

A essa hora Josefa já tinha ido embora e minha mãe estava na cozinha preparando o jantar, que seria salada com frango grelhado (ela estava de dieta, logo todos estávamos também).

Escuto o motor do carro do meu pai, logo desço para recebê-lo, lhe dou um abraço daqueles, e peço ajudar no dever do colégio.

- Pai, pai!! Me ajuda com a matemática mais tarde? – perguntei a ele.

- Claro, filho!! Depois do **jantar** a gente vê isso. – ele respondeu.

- Beleza!!!

Todos nos sentamos à mesa para o jantar que apesar de ser saudável estava muito gostoso. Meu pai sobe para tomar banho e depois vai até meu quarto me ajudar com o dever. Ao final, meus irmãos entram no quarto e começamos uma verdadeira guerra de travesseiros. Nossa, foi muito divertido! Meu pai sempre foi um grande amigo.

Minha mãe manda que todos parem com a **bagunça**, mas assim que paramos ela nos joga dois travesseiros e entra na brincadeira.

Ah, eu **amo** minha família.

Resumo da história

Jorge é um dos filhos de uma grande família. Toda semana divide com seus irmãos as tarefas da casa. Vai à escola todos os dias e às vezes joga bola com os colegas no campinho perto de sua casa. Mesmo com toda a rotina diária, Jorge sabe que tem sorte em ter uma família unida.

Summary of the story

George is one of the children of a large family. Every week he shares with his brothers the chores of the house. He goes to school every day and sometimes plays ball with his colleagues on the playground near his house. Even with all the daily routine, Gorge knows he is lucky to have a united family.

Vocabulary

- **moram:** live
- **irmão:** brother
- **gêmeo:** twin
- **banheiros:** bathrooms
- **quintal:** yard
- **joelho:** knee
- **lixeira:** trash bin
- **tarefas:** tasks
- **flexíveis:** flexible
- **acordo:** wake up
- **tomar banho:** to take a shower
- **me vestir:** to get dressed
- **café da manhã:** breakfast
- **suco de laranja:** orange juice
- **sempre:** always
- **preste atenção:** pay attention
- **ônibus:** bus
- **lava roupa:** do the laundry
- **passar aspirador:** vacuum
- **lavar as mãos:** to wash the hands
- **bife:** steak
- **dever de casa:** homework
- **jogar bola:** play ball (soccer)
- **futebol:** soccer
- **brincando:** playing
- **sujo:** dirty
- **chuveiro:** shower
- **jantar:** dnner
- **bagunça:** mess
- **amo:** love

Questions about the story

1. **Os irmãos de Jorge:**
   a. São um casal de gêmeos
   b. São um casal
   c. São trigêmeos
   d. São dois irmãos

2. **Jorge é responsável por:**
   a. varrer o quintal diariamente
   b. lavar um dos banheiros diariamente
   c. colocar o lixo na lixeira diariamente
   d. lavar a louça toda noite

3. **Os pais de Jorge:**
   a. trabalham apenas de manhã
   b. trabalham de segunda à sexta
   c. trabalham à noite
   d. trabalham, mas o horário do pai é flexível

4. **A moça que faz faxina na casa:**
   a. lava os banheiros, põe o lixo para fora e faz comida
   b. faz comida, passa roupa, lava os banheiros e lav a roupa
   c. lava roupa, passa roupa e coloca comida para o cachorro
   d. faz todas as tarefas da casa

5. **Jorge ficou:**
   a. mais de três horas brincando
   b. mais de uma hora brincando
   c. mais de duas horas brincando
   d. menos de duas horas brincando

Answers

1. A
2. C
3. B
4. B
5. C

CHAPTER NINETEEN

GOING SHOPPING

Quatro amigas à procura de um jeans perfeito – Four friends looking for the perfect jeans

O ano era de **despedidas**, e éramos quatro amigas **inseparáveis** e cheias de histórias para contar, nos conhecemos ainda no colégio e hoje estávamos vivendo o **dilema** de nos despedir de nossa pequena cidade. Duas de nós (Helena e Paty) iam cursar faculdade fora da cidade, eu (Lulu) ia fazer um ano de **intercâmbio** pela África e Cecília ia ser a única **permanecer** no local com seus pais.

Para tanto, decidimos escolher os **vestidos** da formatura do colégio juntas, então não exista nada melhor do que ir ao shopping e às lojas mais badaladas da cidade. Como proveito decidimos por uma ideia **inusitada** (minha) comprar uma peça de roupa idêntica somente com o tamanho diferente para sempre lembrarmos daquele dia único.

Partimos para o Park Shopping, o mais popular da cidade que tinha mais de duzentas lojas, sendo umas trinta somente para **vestuário** feminino, mas também tinha lojas de **sapatos**, **perfumes**, **livrarias**, etc. Helena como sempre adorou, sua diversão de quase todas as tardes era passear no shopping.

- Meninas, nossa tarde será fantástica. Lembra quando vínhamos ao shopping depois das provas trimestrais? Sempre tinha um **filme** legal no cinema e acabávamos o dia comprando doces naquela megaloja ao lado dos fast foods, quem lembra? – disse Helena toda sorridente.

- Hahaha, como posso esquecer? Você tinha aquela queda pelo rapaz que vendia **pipoca** no cinema, sempre comprava um pacote enorme e **nunca** comia tudo!!! – disse Cecília rindo de Helena.

- Ah, Cecília!! Não me faça lembrar daquela vez em que fomos naquele shopping próximo a sua casa que só tinha lojas caras, Dior, Chanel...! Eu não consegui comprar nem um botão naquele lugar. – **retrucou** Helena.

- Gente!! Olhem aquela loja de vestidos! Vamos lá **averiguar** se achamos alguma coisa legal. Nossa, essa loja é nova? Nunca havia reparado. – disse Paty.

Caminhamos todas na maior conversa muito felizes de estarmos juntas naquele shopping. Quando entramos na loja as opções de vestido eram **inúmeras** e resolvemos experimentar vários.

Paty ficou lindíssima com um vestido **vermelho**, só faltava comprar a **sandália** certa; Helena escolheu um com renda branca, muito bonito; Cecília sempre escolhia algo preto, pois dizia que **emagrecia**, apesar dela não estar acima do peso; e eu me apaixonei por um cor de prata, lindíssimo, tinha que achar o sapato e **bolsa** perfeitos para usá-lo.

Saímos da loja cheias de sacolas; aproveitei que estava tudo em **promoção** e comprei presentes para meus pais, afinal eles ficariam um ano sem me ver. Fiquei impressionada com Cecília, saiu com mais sacolas que todas nós juntas, fiquei surpresa, pois ela sempre foi a mais contida.

- Amigas, comprei muita coisa, né? Podem falar a **verdade**. Ando muito ansiosa, porque vou ficar sozinha nessa cidade!!! – disse Cecília.

Nesse momento todas ficamos sentidas e nos abraçamos, deixando cair todas as sacolas e novamente rimos muito daquela situação. Tentamos acalmá-la, afinal, eu voltaria após um ano e as meninas sempre tentarão **manter contato** e iremos nos visitar a cada dois anos, essa era nossa promessa.

Ao passar pelo cinema vímos o rapaz ao qual Helena sempre foi **apaixonada**, e resolvemos dar uma olhada nos filmes em cartaz, por sorte tinha um filme que estava querendo assistir e consegui convencer a todas de assistirmos juntas.

A sessão já ia iniciar então compramos rapidamente os **ingressos** e corremos para a sala de exibição, mas dona Helena fez questão de ir comprar pipoca junto ao tal rapaz, foi nessa hora que fiquei surpreendida, o rapaz pediu o telefone de Helena e disse que sempre a observou. Esse shopping hoje está dando o que falar. Ela ficou toda feliz e disse que seria seu último dia na cidade.

O filme foi ótimo, contava a história de uma moça obcecada por fazer compras, de todo tipo, com vários **cartões de crédito**, comprava sapatos, roupas, inclusive uma barraca de acampamento ela comprou, até se endividar toda e se meter na maior confusão, foi superdivertido. Bem parecido com o que estávamos fazendo naquele dia.

- Eii, estamos esquecendo da nossa peça única, o que vai ser? Uma calça, bolsa, blusa, maquiagem? O que vamos comprar?? – lembrou Paty.

- É verdade! Podemos comprar um perfume igual. – disse Helena.

- Não, você gosta daqueles com **cheiro doce**, eu prefiro os marcantes! Não vai dar certo. – disse para Helena.

- Podemos dar uma olhada nas lojas de joias? – disse Cecília. – Brincadeira, gente! Era só para ver a reação de vocês. Já comprei demais, a única coisa que falta para mim é uma calça! As minhas estão muito velhas.

- Isso!!! Uma calça jeans!! – gritamos as quatro ao mesmo tempo.

- Já sei, aquela loja *Mimada* está em promoção, vamos correndo para lá! – disse Helena.

Em busca da loja que Helena recomendou andamos quase o shopping **inteiro**, no caminho compramos sorvete, rimos muito sobre o ocorrido no cinema e fizemos planos para o futuro. A nostalgia já estava tomando conta de nossos principais assuntos. Aquele shopping era um ótimo ponto de encontro, muito grande, divertido e **aconchegante**.

Achamos a tão falada loja, entramos e – pasmem - estava tudo revirado, acredito que a promoção realmente deu certo, estava uma bagunça! Começamos a procurar as calças e até achamos algumas legais, porém não tinha quatro unidades do mesmo modelo, mesmo dois números sendo diferentes dos demais.

Saímos da loja **tristes**, pois não achamos a calça perfeita. Andando mais um pouco, avistei uma pequena loja chamada Luz de Sol.

- Olha, vamos dar uma olhada naquela dali? – apontei para a loja.

- Ai, parece meio cafona, mas se você quiser podemos ir. – disse Helena.

- Eu gostei, acho que sou **cafona** então! – Cecilia disse morrendo de rir.

- Vamos lá!! – disse para todas.

Decidimos entrar, a fachada da loja era muito bonita e não aparentava ser tão cara. Apesar de Helena ter achado brega, eu achei bem bonita e arrumada. Ao entrarmos fomos recebidas por uma moça muito simpática.

- Bem-vindas a nossa loja, posso ajudar a achar a peça **perfeita**? – disse a atendente.

Todas fizemos aquele olhar surpreso e falamos novamente juntas que precisávamos de uma calça perfeita. A moça até levou um **susto** e riu muito de nós, mas logo nos levou para a parte das calças.

Lá tinham **diversas** opções, de todas as **cores** e **tipos**. Paty que sempre era a mais **tímida** e nunca expressava muito sua opinião, se apaixonou por uma calça jeans clara.

- Gente, olhem esta calça, que tecido gostoso e muito bonita, vamos experimentar essa!! – disse Paty toda animada.

Perguntamos para a moça se tinha todos os tamanhos e quantidade que precisávamos e, sim, tinha os **tamanhos**, só restava experimentar. No provador conseguimos ver que a calça ficou ótima em todas e estava com um preço bem bacana.

Ao sair da loja estávamos muito felizes e realizadas, pois cumprimos todos os objetivos daquele dia que, aliás, foi maravilhoso e **divertido** como nunca! Pode parecer fútil, mas ir até aquele shopping era importante para nós, o tempo que passamos ali foi demais! Nunca vou **esquecer** esse dia e acho que nem as meninas.

Resumo da história

Elas são quatro amigas de infância que vão se separar momentaneamente após a formatura. Por isso, foram escolher os vestidos de formatura e passar alguns últimos momentos juntas, antes da viagem. Para lembrarem umas das outras e da promessa de viajarem para se encontrar, resolveram comprar algo do mesmo modelo para todas.

Summary of the story

They are four childhood friends who will be separated momentarily after graduation. So, they chose the prom dresses and spend some last moments together before the trip. To remember each other and the promise to travel to meet, they decided to buy something of the same model for all of them.

Vocabulary

- **despedidas:** farewells
- **inseparáveis:** inseparable
- **dilema:** dilemma
- **intercâmbio:** exchange
- **permanecer:** to stay
- **vestidos:** dresses
- **inusitada:** unusual
- **vestuário:** clothing
- **sapatos:** shoes
- **perfumes:** perfumes
- **livrarias:** bookstores
- **filme:** movie
- **pipoca:** popcorn
- **nunca:** never
- **retrucou:** replied back
- **averiguar:** to check
- **caminhamos:** walked
- **inúmeras:** countless
- **vermelho:** red
- **sandália:** sandals
- **emagrecia:** looked thinner
- **bolsa:** purse

- **promoção:** promotion
- **verdade:** truth
- **manter contato:** to keep contact
- **apaixonada:** in love
- **ingressos:** tickets
- **cartões de crédito:** credit cards
- **cheiro doce:** sweet smell
- **inteiro:** whole
- **aconchegante:** comfortable
- **tristes:** sad
- **cafona:** of bad taste
- **perfeita:** perfect
- **susto:** scare
- **diversas:** many
- **cores:** colors
- **tipos:** kinds
- **tímida:** shy
- **tamanhos:** sizes
- **divertido:** funny
- **esquecer:** to forget

Questions about the story

1. Helena tinha uma queda:

    a. pelo rapaz que vendia pipoca

    b. pelo rapaz que vendia os ingressos

    c. pelo rapaz que vendia calças

    d. pelo rapaz que vendia livros

2. Cecília escolheu o vestido:

    a. com renda branca, muito bonito

    b. vermelho, sem a sandália

    c. prata, lindíssimo

    d. preto, pois emagrece

3. No filme que as amigas assistiram, a personagem principal era obcecada:

    a. por comida

    b. por rapazes

    c. por compras

    d. por viagens

4. A peça em comum que as amigas combinaram de comprar era:

    a. maquiagem

    b. uma calça

    c. uma joia

    d. um perfume

5. Helena disse que a loja era:

    a. brega

    b. bonita e arrumada

    c. cara

    d. cafona

Answers

1. A
2. D
3. C
4. B
5. D

CHAPTER TWENTY

BASIC VOCABULARY PART 2

Vamos à praia? – Shall we go to the beach?

No **verão** dá **vontade** de ir à praia, tomar **banho de sol**, pisar descalço na **areia**, mergulhar no **mar** salgado, e tudo isso sempre me lembrava das minhas idas e vindas da **praia** de Itacoatiara. Estava preparando uma viagem para um lugar paradisíaco ao qual ainda não conhecia: a **reserva ambiental** Ilha Grande. Lá existem diversas praias, algumas remotas outras, com destaque para sua água azul e diversidade **marinha**.

Minhas férias se iniciam em dois dias, tempo suficiente para fazer as malas e deixar tudo em ordem até o meu retorno. Dessa vez estava **solteira** então iria sozinha mesmo, adoro viajar e não ter companhia confirmada nunca é um **problema**.

Chega o dia da viagem. Para chegar até lá tive que pegar uma **balsa** que fica a uma hora e meia da minha casa, embarco uma das primeiras que saem do **cais**. Sinto-me muito empolgada. Ainda na balsa já conheço uma **família**, um casal com seus três filhos pequenos.

- Olá, primeira vez em Ilha Grande? – pergunta a mãe dos meninos.

- Sim, primeira. Estou muito empolgada para conhecer tudo, ou quase tudo. E vocês?

- Não, deve ser nossa quinta vez, adoramos a ilha, as pessoas, as praias, os passeios. Tudo é maravilhoso nesse **pedaço** de chão ou melhor dizendo, de mar. – disse o pai da família.

- Como se chamam, esqueci de perguntar. – pergunto aos familiares.

- Eu sou Maria, meu marido se chama Eduardo e esses são nossos três filhos, Luiza, Alan e Thiago, todos amam passar as férias na ilha. E o seu nome, qual é? Já tem pousada para ficar? – disse a mãe da família.

- Sou Valentina, mais todos me chamam de Tina. Eu **reservei** uma pousada chamada, Sol e Lua, é boa? – respondo.

Logo as crianças se empolgam, estávamos indo inclusive para a mesma pousada, segundo eles, uma das **melhores** da ilha. Assim que a balsa **atraca** no porto da Vila do Abraão, pegamos nossas malas e juntos vamos até a pousada.

Na parte da frente tinha um rapaz com um cachorro lindíssimo esperando por nós. O Zé iria **ajudar** com as malas e nos **orientar** sobre o que fazer na ilha, quer dizer, orientar só a mim, a família já estava tranquila em seu roteiro.

- Dona Tina, posso te apresentar um rapaz que faz passeios de barco magníficos, existem algumas praias que você só chega de barco de tão **exclusivas** que são. Outra coisa, próximo à pousada você já encontra uma praia logo a sua frente e ao redor temos ótimos **restaurantes**. – disse Zé.

- Poxa, que legal. Existem alguns passeios que podem incluir grupos diferentes, gostaria de conhecer mais pessoas na ilha, seria divertido. À noite tem alguma **atração** na Vila? – perguntei a ele.

- Claro, no período da noite temos o **centro da cidade**, com **barracas** que vendem comidas típicas, roupas de praia, alguns quiosques com cerveja gelada e guloseimas, e também existem os bares, são um pouco mais caros, mas sempre tem **música ao vivo** e boa comida. Bom, opção é o que não falta. – disse Zé. – Vou indo, Tina, qualquer coisa aqui está o número do meu celular para contato.

- Muito obrigada pelas dicas, Zé. Vou fazer tudo como me disse, agora mesmo irei almoçar naquele restaurante famoso por sua peixada fresca. – agradeço ao Zé.

- **Por nada**, divirta-se! – despediu-se Zé.

Nesse momento entro no meu **quarto**, muito simpático por sinal, cama confortável, **televisão** funcionando, o banheiro também parece ser ótimo. Mas minha barriga não me deixa esquecer que estou com muita fome. Visto uma roupa mais praiana e vou até o restaurante.

Chego ao lugar que tanto ouvi falar, por meio dos **moradores**, do casal que acabara de conhecer e da internet... muitos elogios. Sento em uma mesa de frente para o mar e logo tiro uma foto e envio para minha mãe, que adorou o visual!

- Oi, **garçom**, tudo bem? Gostaria de saber qual o prato que mais sai no horário do almoço? – pergunto ao garçom mais próximo.

- Olá, moça bonita! Hoje posso indicar nossa caldeirada, uma mistura de camarões, lulas, pescado, tudo em um caldo maravilhoso, que tal? – disse o garçom.

- Fiquei com água na boca, pode pedir uma porção individual, por favor! E para beber traga uma cerveja gelada. – faço o pedido.

- Feito, já, já o pedido chega.

A visão em minha frente é **magnífica**, o mar é lindo demais e o ambiente também é muito bacana. Resolvi que iria conhecer duas praias naquele dia e converso por **mensagens** no celular com o amigo do Zé, o rapaz que faz passeios de barco. Combinamos de nos encontrar daqui a duas horas no cais em frente à pousada.

O almoço chega e realmente é **delicioso**, nunca comi uma caldeirada igual àquela - e olha que adoro **frutos do mar**! Após o almoço vou até o meu quarto preparar minha mochila para o passeio, coloco coisas básicas, biquíni extra, protetor solar, toalhas e algum lanchinho.

Felipe (o rapaz do barco) **está a minha espera** com um grupo de mais quatro pessoas, todos viajantes solitários como eu. Entro no barco e me apresento ao pessoal, que de prontidão faz o mesmo, até americano tinha na excursão!

- Boa tarde, pessoal! Sou a Tina, vamos conhecer algumas praias hoje? Pegar um solzinho? Ficar bronzeados? – digo ao pessoal do barco.

- Opa, vamos sim! Hoje será maravilhoso. – disse José, um dos rapazes do grupo.

- Hoje o dia está favorável, vamos poder aproveitar bastante! – disse Amanda, outra integrante do grupo.

Essa hora Felipe já está com o barco em **movimento**. Nosso primeiro destino é a praia do Dentista, sem bares, sem cadeiras de praia, apenas um visual paradisíaco. Atracamos próximo à praia e descemos para tomar banho de mar. Chegando à areia é muito bom contemplar todo aquele visual. Tiramos muitas fotos, conversamos bastante, enfim, a praia era maravilhosa. Não entendi o significado do nome, mas ninguém soube explicar.

Após umas duas horas naquela praia partimos ruma a praia dos Coqueiros, famosa por ser a praia dos surfistas e que possui um coqueiro que cresceu de maneira inesperada e entortou, causando um enorme **efeito visual**. Demais!

- Felipe, você sabe por que a praia se chama "Coqueiros"? – perguntei ao guia.

- Essa eu sei, justamente por ser dominada por eles, os coqueiros, lá existem muitos e de todos os formatos, é muito legal! – responde o guia.

Chegando à praia dos Coqueiros que estava um pouco mais cheia por ser mais famosa que a anterior o horizonte é **fenomenal**, uma coisa linda! Sinto-me em casa nessas horas, com uma liberdade imensa, acho muito bom desfrutar de minha própria companhia.

Fico na areia da praia tomando banho de sol e admirando toda aquela paisagem. De repente, me pego pensando: se esse é o primeiro dia imagine os que estão por vir!

Resumo da história

Valentina está viajando sozinha para uma Ilha onde muitas aventuras a esperam. Ela inicia a viagem fazendo novas amizades, experimentando novas comidas e experienciando conhecer lugares em que nunca imaginou estar.

Summary of the story

Valentina is traveling alone to an Island where many adventures await her. She begins the journey by making new friends, experimenting new food and experiencing places she has never imagined.

Vocabulary

- **verão:** summer
- **vontade:** will
- **banho de sol:** sunbath
- **areia:** sand
- **mar:** sea
- **praia:** beach
- **reserva ambiental:** environmental reserve
- **marinha:** marine
- **solteira:** single
- **problema:** problem
- **balsa:** ferry
- **cais:** pier
- **família:** family
- **pedaço:** piece
- **reservei:** reserved
- **melhores:** best
- **atraca:** dock
- **ajudar:** to help
- **orientar:** to guide
- **exclusivas:** exclusive
- **restaurantes:** restaurants
- **atração:** attraction
- **centro da cidade:** city center
- **barracas:** tents
- **música ao vivo:** live music
- **por nada:** you're welcome
- **quarto:** room
- **televisão:** TV
- **moradores:** residents
- **garçom:** waiter
- **magnífica:** magnificent
- **mensagens:** messages
- **delicioso:** delicious
- **futos do mar:** seafood
- **está a minha espera:** waiting for me
- **movimento:** movement
- **efeito visual:** visual effect
- **fenomenal:** phenomenal

Questions about the story

1. **O lugar pra viajar era:**
    a. com diversidade botânica
    b. água verde
    c. paradisíaco e desconhecido
    d. com diversidade animal

2. **Para chegar até a Ilha Grande Tina precisa:**
    a. pegar um avião por duas horas e meia
    b. pegar uma balsa por uma hora e meia
    c. pegar um ônibus por uma hora e meia
    d. pegar um táxi por duas horas e meia

3. **Tina se hospeda em uma pousada chamada:**
    a. Sol e Lua
    b. Sol e nuvem
    c. Nuvem e Lua
    d. Sol e chuva

4. **Para o almoço, o garçom indica:**
    a. feijoada com toucinho
    b. caldeirada com frutos do mar
    c. rabada com batatas
    d. bacalhoada com caldo

5. **No passeio de barco, quais são os primeiros destinos?**
    a. Praia do florista e praia dos Coqueiros
    b. Praia dos Coqueiros e praia do Dentista
    c. Praia do Dentista e praia dos Coqueiros
    d. Praia dos Coqueiros e praia do Florista

Answers

1. C
2. B
3. A
4. B
5. C

CONCLUSION

Hello again, reader!

We hope you've enjoyed our stories and the way we've presented them. Each chapter, as you will have noticed, was a way to practice a language tool which you will regularly use when speaking Portuguese. Whether it's verbs, pronouns or simple conversations, the Portuguese tongue has a great essence of grammar which can be just as challenging to learn as it can be entertaining.

Never forget: learning a language doesn't *have* to be a boring activity if you find the proper way to do it. Hopefully we've provided you with a hands-on, fun way to expand your knowledge in Portuguese and you can apply your lessons to future ventures.

Feel free to use this book further ahead when you need to go back to remembering vocabulary and expressions — in fact, we encourage it.

Believe in yourself and never be ashamed to make mistakes. Even the best can fall; it's those who get up that can achieve greatness! Take care!

PS: Keep an eye out for more books like this one; we're not done teaching you Portuguese! Head over to www.LingoMastery.com and read our free articles, sign up for our newsletter and check out our Youtube channel. We give away so much free stuff that will accelerate your Portuguese learning and you don't want to miss that!

Take care and until next time!

MORE BOOKS BY LINGO MASTERY

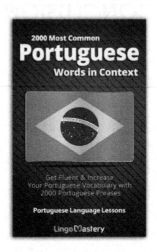

Have you been trying to learn Portuguese and simply can't find the way to expand your vocabulary?

Do your teachers recommend you boring textbooks and complicated stories that you don't really understand?

Are you looking for a way to learn the language quicker without taking shortcuts?

If you answered "Yes!" to at least one of those previous questions, then this book is for you! We've compiled the **2000 Most Common Words in Portuguese**, a list of terms that will expand your vocabulary to levels previously unseen.

Did you know that — according to an important study — learning the top two thousand (2000) most frequently used words will enable you to understand up to **84%** of all non-fiction and **86.1%** of fiction literature and **92.7%** of oral speech? Those are amazing stats, and this book will take you even further than those numbers!

In this book:

- A detailed introduction with tips and tricks on how to improve your learning
- A list of 2000 of the most common words in Portuguese and their translations
- An example sentence for each word – in both Portuguese and English
- Finally, a conclusion to make sure you've learned and supply you with a final list of tips

Don't look any further, we've got what you need right here!

In fact, we're ready to turn you into a Portuguese speaker... are you ready to get involved in becoming one?

Made in the USA
Las Vegas, NV
20 January 2021

16230032R00115